THE BALLYCOTTON JOB

AN INCREDIBLE TRUE STORY OF IRA PIRATES

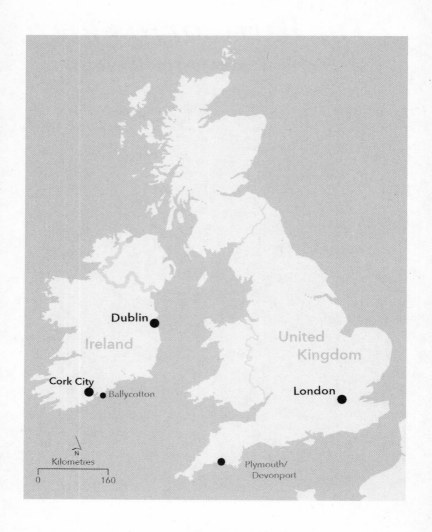

IRELAND AND BRITAIN

THE BALLYCOTTON JOB

AN INCREDIBLE TRUE STORY OF IRA PIRATES

Tom Mahon

To Peter with Aloha

Tom Mahon

MERCIER PRESS

DEDICATION
For Sui Lan and Tommy

MERCIER PRESS

Cork

www.mercierpress.ie

Cover design: Sarah O'Flaherty

© Tom Mahon, 2022

ISBN 978-1-78117-443-2
ISBN 978-1-78117-444-9 E Book

A CIP record for this title is available from the British Library.

Printed and bound in the EU.

CONTENTS

ACKNOWLEDGMENTS

Researching and writing this book has been a most enjoyable marathon, over the course of which I've visited numerous archives and historical sites. The project came together one piece at a time until I ended up uncovering far more information than I ever expected. One thing that I can attest to is that truth is indeed stranger than fiction.

I've endeavoured not just to tell a fascinating adventure story, but also to peel away the layers that obscure the underlying characters, to look at the nature of violence and prejudice, to cast light on the subjectivity of views on morality and justice and to consider the difficulty of distinguishing perpetrators from victims and vice versa. Where possible I've given the full name of fatalities, even if their deaths are only mentioned in passing, in order to commemorate their lives and the tragedy of their deaths. Colonialism and the attitudes associated with it play an important role in this narrative and likewise I believe they were significant factors in the War of Independence that remain under-appreciated to this day.

I'm deeply indebted to countless archivists, librarians, local historians and experts. To all of those whom I've inadvertently failed to acknowledge, I sincerely apologise.

I'm especially grateful to two outstanding historians for sharing their knowledge, insights and time: Dr John Borgonovo of University College Cork and Prof. Peter Hoffenberg of the University of Hawaii.

I was delighted to be able to make contact with the descendants of some of the participants. It's been a pleasure meeting Len Williams, grandson and namesake of the captain of the *Warrior*. I'm grateful to Len for sharing a trove of documentation and images about his grandfather, a brave and skilful tugboat captain who saved scores of lives during the First World War.

This story would never have occurred were it not for the brilliant Captain Jeremiah Collins – a true Irish patriot – and so it was terrific to hear from his great-great granddaughter Rachel Wheeler and her mother Noreen Kinney. I appreciate being able to look at their fabulous collection of photographs and newspaper clippings.

I was fortunate to correspond with Bob Long and David Kerr, two experts on historic tugboats. Len and I visited the *Challenge*, a restored steam tugboat in Southampton, where we spent the day with David. This was one of the highlights of my research. The *Challenge* is a beautiful vessel (similar to the *Warrior*); you can learn more about her and support her preservation at *stchallenge.org*. Thank you David and Bob for your great work.

I'd also like to thank the following.

UCD Archives – especially Seamus Helferty (retired), principal archivist Kate Manning and Selina Collard. The A-Team at Cork Archives Institute, Brian McGee archivist and Michael and Peter. Commandant Victor Lange (retired) and the staff at the Military Archives, Dublin. Mary Horgan, Gerry Desmond and John Mullins of Cork City Library. Dan Breen curator of Cork Public Museum.

A special thanks to the staff at the National Archives in Kew including Michael from Dublin.

Stuart McMahon, of the website Clyde Maritime, an excellent resource for the history of shipping on the Clyde and to Colin Campbell. Terence Smith of *rifleman.org.uk* who sent me information about historical military ammunition. Chris White of Historical RFA (Royal Fleet Auxiliary) website, who sent me his essay on the capture of the *Upnor* along with important archival documents. Noreen Brennan, Michael Martin and Aidan Murphy of Met Éireann. Christine Fernon, online manager of the Australian Dictionary of Biography. Dr Lynsey Robertson of the Churchill Archives Centre.

Aidan O'Sullivan, Niall Murray and Deirdre Bourke of the Kilmurry Historical and Archaeological Association.

Local historians John Hennessey and Mike Deane shared their extensive knowledge on Cobh/Queenstown in 1922. Kieran McCarthy, author of *Republican Cobh and the East Cork Volunteers*, the preeminent expert on the history of the Cobh IRA. Many thanks to the sisters of Saint Benedict's, Cobh who let me visit their priory, which was once Admiralty House; thank you for your gracious hospitality. Yvonne Allen curator at Cobh Museum. Mary O'Donovan and Stan Reynolds in Cobh. Tom O'Neill historian and author of *The Battle of Clonmult*. James Cronin of the beautiful Gregans Castle Hotel, where Louise Gaunt's family was from. Fr Richard Flanagan in Ballyvaughan.

Thanks to John Stratton in Waterford and Miriam McSweeney of the Galway-Mayo Institute of Technology. My sister Anne in Heidelberg and Paul Kuramoto and

Michael Flumian in Honolulu. Tommy Mahon – a poet and scholar – who edited some of the chapters. As always thanks to Mary Feehan and her team at Mercier.

The maps were created by the multi-talented Charlie Roche of MobileGIS Ltd. A geographer, researcher and cartographer Charlie has previously contributed to the stunning *Atlas of the Great Irish Famine* and *Atlas of the Irish Revolution* (both published by Cork University Press).

This book was written with fond memories of the wonderful Crofts family: Dominic and Deirdre, Helen and my mother Mary as well as Tom and Ellen. My grandfather Tom was one of the team that seized the *Upnor*.

Tom Mahon, Honolulu, 2022

GLOSSARY

Anglo-Irish Treaty: Treaty negotiated between representatives of the British and Dáil cabinets in December 1921. It led to self-rule with the establishment of the Irish Free State.

Anti-Treaty IRA: IRA units that opposed the Treaty. Also referred to as 'republicans' and 'irregulars' (by the Free State).

Auxiliaries: The Auxiliary Division of the RIC, known as Auxies. Frequently and incorrectly referred to as Black and Tans. A heavily armed paramilitary force comprising ex-British army officers that was operationally independent of the RIC. Though prone to unauthorised reprisals, it posed a formidable threat to the IRA.

Black and Tans: Colloquial term for members of the RIC recruited from ex-soldiers in Britain. They had a reputation for indiscipline, drunkenness and brutality.

Brigade: A key organisational unit of the IRA, comprising a thousand or more volunteers. Cork had three brigades throughout much of the War of Independence.

Cork: The largest Irish county as well as the name of the principal city in the south. In the War of Independence, it witnessed the heaviest fighting and the most casualties. During the Civil War, it was a stronghold of the anti-Treaty IRA.

Cork No. 1 Brigade: One of the IRA's largest and most effective units. Its area of operations included the city and a large swath of the countryside, extending from

Youghal in the east to Ballyvourney in the west. Seán O'Hegarty assumed command in the autumn of 1920.

Dáil: Independent and initially clandestine Irish parliament formed in Dublin in January 1919 by members of Sinn Féin, who were originally elected to the House of Commons in London. It became the legislature for the Free State. The Dáil elected its own separatist cabinet.

Devonport: A district of Plymouth and the site of the Royal Navy dockyards, one of the navy's largest and most important facilities.

Easter Rising: Abortive Irish insurrection in Dublin in 1916 led by the Irish Volunteers and the IRB. It was a military failure, but it spurred the reorganisation of the Volunteers and the War of Independence.

Flying Column: IRA unit composed of full-time volunteers on the run. Columns were mainly based in the countryside, and tended to be well-armed and mobile.

GHQ: General Headquarters. The secret IRA headquarters in Dublin. Nominally under the command of Risteárd Mulcahy, but in effect led by Michael Collins.

Great War: In its aftermath the First World War was commonly referred to as the Great War both in Britain and Ireland.

Hegarty's Crowd: Also known as the 'irregulars' or the 'active squad'. A small group of fighters within Cork No. 1 Brigade, who were members of the IRB and were personally loyal to Seán O'Hegarty. They were responsible for much of the ambushes and shootings in the city.

Home Rule: A limited degree of self-government for Ireland, which was supported by moderate Irish nationalists and the Liberal Party in Great Britain.

IRA: Irish Republican Army. Force committed to fighting for an independent republic and ostensibly allegiant to the Dáil. Members often called themselves 'volunteers' while the British frequently called them 'Shinners'.

IRB: Irish Republican Brotherhood, popularly known as the Fenian movement. Secretive revolutionary group that maintained considerable influence over the IRA and Sinn Féin.

Irish Civil War: Conflict between the anti-Treaty IRA and the pro-Treaty National Army from June 1922 to May 1923. Resulted in a victory of the National Army for the Free State.

Irish Free State: Self-governing state established after the Anglo-Irish Treaty; it was officially inaugurated in December 1922. Ireland (with the exception of six counties in the north-east) achieved a degree of independence equivalent to a dominion, but short of a fully sovereign republic.

Irish Volunteers: Nationalist militia formed in 1913 and together with the IRB responsible for the Easter Rising of 1916. By 1919, it became known as the IRA.

Loyalist: Person loyal to the British crown and the union of Britain and Ireland. Loyalists formed a majority in the north-east, but were in an overall minority on the island.

National Army: From early 1922 the pro-Treaty IRA began to be known as the National Army, with Michael Collins as commander-in-chief.

OC: Officer commanding.

Provisional Government: A transitional Irish administration formed by pro-Treaty members of Sinn Féin in January 1922 with Michael Collins as chairman. It lasted until the official establishment of the Free State in December 1922.

Pro-Treaty IRA: IRA units, which supported Michael Collins and the Treaty. Reorganised as the National Army.

Queenstown: The principal port in Cork harbour, it was renamed Cobh during the War of Independence, though the former name persisted for several years. Headquarters of the Royal Navy in Ireland, as well as the leading port in Ireland for transatlantic shipping.

RIC: Royal Irish Constabulary. Armed police force. Initially composed of Irish constables, but having come close to collapse during the War of Independence it was reinforced with British recruits in 1920.

Sinn Féin: Irish nationalist party founded in 1905. In the aftermath of the 1916 Easter Rising, it became the leading separatist party and political partner of the IRA.

Troubles: Euphemistic term for the War of Independence.

Truce: Agreement between representatives of the Dáil cabinet and the British commander-in-chief in Ireland, Gen. Macready, resulting in an armistice on 11 July 1921 in the War of Independence.

Unionist: Synonymous with 'loyalist'.

War of Independence: 1919 to 1921. War between the IRA and the British army and the RIC.

Key Characters

Tom Barry: Leader of the IRA's West Cork flying column. He was a well-known, arrogant and brilliant guerrilla fighter who led the Kilmichael ambush of December 1920, which annihilated an Auxiliary patrol of eighteen officers.

Winston Churchill: As Secretary of State for War (1919 to 1921) and for the Colonies (1921 to 1922) he was the senior British cabinet minister most involved with Irish affairs.

Jeremiah Collins: Cork merchant and ship's captain, who smuggled weapons and sheltered fugitives for the IRA. A supporter of the Free State, he regarded the anti-Treaty IRA as too extreme.

Michael Collins: Director of Intelligence of the IRA, President of the IRB and Minister of Finance in the Dáil government. He was chief of the IRA during the War of Independence and following the Treaty became chairman of the pro-Treaty Provisional Government and commander-in-chief of the National Army.

Admiral Sir Ernest Gaunt: Commander of the Royal Navy in Ireland and based in Queenstown.

David Lloyd George: British Prime Minister, 1916–1922.

Gen. Sir Nevil Macready: General Officer Commanding in Chief of the British Army in Ireland.

Risteárd Mulcahy: Chief of Staff of the IRA and Collins' principal deputy.

Seán O'Hegarty: Commander of Cork No. 1 Brigade,

known for his bravery and ruthlessness. He became a prominent leader of the anti-Treaty IRA.

Dan 'Sandow' O'Donovan: One of O'Hegarty's key officers.

Gen. Sir Peter Strickland: Officer Commanding the 6th Division. In charge of the British army in southern Ireland, with his headquarters at Victoria Barracks in Cork city.

DIALOGUE

The vast majority of the dialogue is based on primary sources such as interviews and statements by the characters themselves. In the immediate aftermath of the operation the Royal Navy questioned the crews of the *Upnor* and the *Warrior*, while members of the IRA were later interviewed by their comrade Ernie O'Malley, made statements to the Bureau of Military History in Dublin, and or talked to newspaper journalists and historians. I have accessed all these records. For further details, see Notes and References, p. 231.

In a small number of situations, I've inserted dialogue based on statements, phrases and words associated with the participants in other situations. For instance in the section where Seán O'Hegarty talked about the plan to seize the *Upnor* to his brigade officers, I took phrases from Bureau of Military History witness statements that he used when sending volunteers out on a dangerous mission as well as observations from one of his comrades, Frank Busteed.

The only sections where there has been limited reconstruction of dialogue are as follows: O'Hegarty talking to his officers about the plan, Sandow O'Donovan and Captain

Collins during the kidnapping, O'Hegarty seeing Sandow and Mick Murphy off from Cork, Sandow's interaction with Mick Burke at the Deepwater Quay, Sandow talking to John Duhig, Duhig's men talking to the cook, Jeremiah Collins talking to Sandow about the ship's whistle, Sandow, Mick Murphy and Jeremiah Collins conferring about the search for the *Upnor* and Sandow talking to Collins on the bridge of the *Warrior* before entering Ballycotton.

One minor caveat is that most of the fighters – especially O'Hegarty, Sandow and Jim Gray – were well known for their use of profanities, which were usually expunged from later statements and memoirs. Florence O'Donoghue remarked on 'O'Hegarty's vigorous and comprehensive command of bad language and I had yet to meet anyone who could excel him when he was thoroughly roused'.

WEIGHTS AND MEASUREMENTS

I have adhered to the metric system for weights and measurements, except when they're included in a contemporary quote or used to classify weaponry, e.g. the three-pounder gun on the *Upnor:*

    1 ton = 1,016 kilograms
    1 pound = 0.45 kilogram
    1 mile = 1.6 kilometres
    1 yard = 0.9 metre
    1 foot = 0.3 metre
    1 inch = 25 millimetre
    1 knot = 1.85 kilometres/hour.

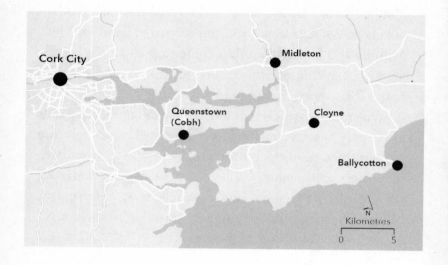

CORK HARBOUR AND
SURROUNDINGS

I

MEDUSA's RETURN

Of the many harbours and bays along the southern coast of Ireland, Cork Harbour is by far the largest and the most scenic. In fact, after Sydney Harbour, it's the largest harbour in the world. The American consul at Queenstown also called it the most beautiful. But aside from its enormous size and natural beauty, it is of great historic and strategic importance.

In the nineteenth and early twentieth centuries, it was the Royal Navy's headquarters in Ireland and a major dockyard and victualling centre for vessels setting out for all corners of the world. During the First World War, a massive fleet of up to thirty-nine American destroyers together with the Royal Navy's warships was based there; entrusted with protecting the vital transatlantic convoys from German submarines lurking in the waters off the Irish coast. In addition Cork was a major port for both merchant and passenger vessels, including those that brought two and a half million impoverished Irish to America in the one hundred years following the Great Famine (1845–49).

Queenstown (now known as Cobh) was its principal deep-water port. It lay seven kilometres opposite the narrow harbour entrance, whereas Cork city was a further thirteen kilometres up-channel to the north-west. The town was built on a steep slope overlooking the water and at the top of the hill was a colonial style mansion, with a large balcony facing out over the ocean. This was Admiralty House, the home of the resident British admiral and his family.

During the turbulent years of the War of Independence and the birth of the Irish Free State Admiral Sir Ernest Gaunt was the naval commander in Queenstown. Following the ratification of the Anglo-Irish Treaty in January 1922, his duties abruptly changed from overseeing naval operations to dismantling most of the navy's bases in Ireland and supervising the army's evacuation. By late March, he had been working for weeks without a break and the strain was beginning to show. Like the other senior British commanders, he was thoroughly sick of Ireland. He regarded the Treaty as a capitulation to the IRA and was looking forward to leaving the God forsaken place. Let the Irish fight it out amongst themselves, to hell with them – he thought.

THURSDAY, 30 MARCH 1922

It is said that how you start your morning sets the tone for the rest of the day and for Gaunt Thursday 30 March got off to a promising start, with no disruption to his well established routine. At eight o'clock, a little after sunrise, he quietly slipped out of bed so as not to disturb his wife, Lady Louise, muttering to himself that the house was miserably cold and draughty.

Having put on his uniform, neatly laid out by his valet the night before, he gingerly descended the narrow staircase to the dining room. Because of a war wound, he walked with a limp and had learned to be careful on the stairs.

Downstairs he glanced out the window. In front of him stretched the broad expanse of the harbour – the sea was dark and calm – there were several vessels at anchor and in the distance he could make out Roches Point lighthouse at the harbour mouth.

The fifty-seven year old looked weary and rumpled, his shoulders slumped and his uniform fitted loosely around his short stature. He wore a navy-blue officer's working uniform; the jacket had two rows of gilded brass buttons, a handkerchief folded into the breast pocket and no epaulettes. On the cuffs were three golden bands, one with a distinctive loop, which signified his rank of vice admiral. With his greying beard and goatee, he bore a striking resemblance to King George V whom he deeply admired.

Ernest no longer had the chiselled profile of his youth; his face had softened and his once fierce eyes had mellowed. There was a time when his glance could instil fear in his subordinates, but nowadays he was more a source of sympathy or even ridicule.

On taking his seat he ate alone: scrambled eggs, bacon (crispy) and kippers along with toast and a pot of tea. It was time for the morning papers. He scoured the *Times*, looking for news about the navy and Ireland and in particular any update on his *bête noir* the First Sea Lord, Admiral Sir David Beatty along with his enabler Winston Churchill, the Secretary of State for the Colonies. How he loathed the pair.

The paper carried a curious article titled 'Cork Kidnapping Case': 'Practically every motor lorry in Cork was commandeered yesterday, it is believed by the Republicans, and driven from the city to an unknown destination. The drivers of the lorries were compelled to accompany the cars. Captain Collins, of the Harbour Commission, a prominent Cork coal merchant, who is a supporter of the Treaty was kidnapped outside a bank in Cork and taken away in a motor car'. But Ernest had become accustomed to the endemic lawlessness and he likely took little if any notice.

Next, he started on the *Cork Constitution*, the local loyalist paper. On first glance, it was the usual news. Michael Collins was in London holding talks with Winston Churchill. At the anti-Treaty IRA convention held over the weekend in Dublin Tom Barry had called for a military dictatorship. There were reports of numerous shootings and robberies, which ever since the ratification of the Treaty were steadily increasing in frequency. The IRA destroyed the printing presses of the pro-Treaty *Freeman's Journal* newspaper in Dublin. In the north, two police constables were shot dead and another wounded. Closer to home there was an attempted robbery of the Hibernian Bank in Cork.

But there were two brief stories that Gaunt would sub-sequently learn were interconnected. On page four was a paragraph titled: 'Lorries taken, an amazing proceeding.' Like the *Times* it mentioned that lorries throughout the city were commandeered and driven 'to unknown rural districts.' However, it was not until he reached the bottom of page six that Gaunt's interest was finally piqued:

HMS Medusa

About midday on Tuesday the naval store ship *Medusa*, which has been sold for breaking-up purposes, left Cork Harbour in tow of a tug for a cross-Channel port. Yesterday, about 10:30 a.m. she was seen entering the harbour again in tow of the same tug, which brought her up past Cobh [*sic*] to her former moorings in Monkstown Bay. The tug *Warrior*, which was engaged in the towage, then came alongside the Deepwater Quay. A number of men went on board and she immediately put to sea at great speed.

Whether Gaunt himself realised the full implication of this piece or whether he needed the advice of his senior naval officer Captain Hugh Sommerville it's impossible to know. The captain, who came from a prominent local Anglo-Irish family, would have been familiar with the comings and goings in Queenstown. Maybe he saw a group of gunmen rush through the streets the previous day, heard a commotion, or more likely he had obtained a snippet of information from a shop keeper or dock worker. But whatever the precise sequence of events, by 10:00 Gaunt knew something terribly serious was afoot.

It was now evident that the IRA had seized the *Warrior*. But of much greater concern to Gaunt was the safety of the *Upnor* and its precious cargo of over a hundred tons (100,000 kilograms) of munitions. The *Upnor* had left Queenstown a few hours before the tugboat, bound for Plymouth.

Unable to get any word of the *Upnor's* whereabouts Gaunt ordered the destroyer *HMS Strenuous* and the sloop *HMS Heather* to 'raise steam for full speed' and search for her. His colleague Admiral Sir Montague Browning in Plymouth dispatched two destroyers to assist. To paraphrase Oscar Wilde: to lose one ship may be regarded as a misfortune; to lose two looks like carelessness.

Gaunt was making history by becoming the first admiral to learn about an enemy attack directed against him from his morning newspaper. He knew something was terribly wrong, but he was unable to make sense of what exactly was unfolding. He was unsure whether the forces of the Provisional Government under Michael Collins or the anti-Treaty IRA were to blame. How could the IRA contemplate such an operation since it was well known that they had no sea going expertise or capability? Did they think they could get away with challenging the mighty Royal Navy?

Not too far away in Ballycotton, Seán O'Hegarty, the IRA commander in Cork city, had a clearer view of what was happening. Victory would put him in a position of unassailable strength, whereas defeat – with the loss of his best fighters – would cripple his brigade.

But we're jumping ahead of ourselves. How did this all come to be?

2

Tremble and Obey

In December 1903, Ernest Gaunt commanded the torpedo cruiser *HMS Mohawk* on a patrol off the coast of Somalia. Beyond the turquoise waters of the Gulf of Aden, he could see the narrow strip of semi-desert scrubland, crossed by dry sandy river beds and in the background loomed the rugged Karkaar Mountains. Settlements dotted the coast, where the villagers eked out a living raising scrawny cattle and goats, fishing and trading. To the fury of the inhabitants, Britain had recently seized the western portion of Somalia as a protectorate and its Italian ally had done likewise in the east.

Gaunt came ashore at the Italian base of Bandar Qassim (now Bosaso) where he was told that two days earlier, Lieut Charles Grabau had been killed at the village of Durbo. Grabau had been shot after he threatened to bombard the village and kidnap its chiefs for refusing to fly the Italian flag.

On hearing the news, the thirty-eight year old Commander Gaunt was determined to avenge the Italian's death. Moreover, he relished the thought of a fight, '[I] wanted to see what it would be like to be under fire and whether [I] would be frightened.'

Deliberately neglecting to telegraph the admiralty in London for further instructions, he hastily set sail and anchoring off Durbo that evening, he waited until daybreak before coming ashore accompanied by sixty armed marines and sailors. With his men covering from the beach, he walked half way to the village to parlay with the two chiefs. Meanwhile a strong force of Somalis dug in and aimed their rifles at the intruders.

Gaunt, declared 'I am the captain of a British man-of-war and we are allies of Italy', before demanding that the chiefs return with him to be handed over to the Italians and that the villagers surrender one hundred rifles. After the pair rebuffed him saying that they needed a delay of six days to consult with their sultan, Gaunt issued an ultimatum and returned to the beach to wait.

According to a – probably exaggerated – British report the Somalis now numbered 400 fighters. Gaunt drew his men into a line with marines to the right and sailors on the left and he stood in the centre beside a large wheeled Maxim machine gun. The Maxim, capable of firing three hundred rounds a minute, was the colonial pacifier par excellence.

After a short interval, the *Mohawk* fired a warning shot and when the Somalis failed to surrender it commenced a barrage with its three-pounder (47 mm calibre) guns; the shells effortlessly wrecking homes, food stores and possessions. Then with a bugle call the English advanced. Gaunt led – revolver in one hand, sword in the other – fearless and resolute. However, within minutes a bullet shattered his thigh bone and he collapsed, critically wounded.

His second in command, Lieut Frank Powell, pressed the attack. After half an hour, the villagers had fled and Powell 'ordered the men to burn and destroy as much of the village as possible'. Finally, the warship covered the British withdrawal by maintaining a heavy bombardment of what remained of Durbo.

Powell estimated that between this skirmish and the earlier fight with the Italians eighty-seven Somalis died, though in all probability the casualties – including women and children – were higher; the sole English fatality was a marine who died, having been shot in the head. It was, in the words of the *Evening Telegraph*, 'a little British fight.'

Ernest was brought to hospital in Aden and although initially not expected to live he obstinately refused to allow the doctors to amputate his leg, which would have ended his naval career. But as he steadily recovered, he became the hero he had always desperately wanted to be. Italian sailors visited to serenade him with operatic tunes and later on his way back to England he stopped off in Rome where King Victor Emmanuel III awarded him the silver *Medaglia al Valore di Marina* (navy valour medal) for 'gallant conduct'. Newspapers throughout England and in his native Australia wrote of his bravery and within a month he was promoted to captain 'for service in the attack on Durbo.'

Almost two years later having declined a pension because of his injuries, he returned to active service, taking command of the cruiser *Cambrian*.

Ernest Frederick Augustus Gaunt was born in 1865, in what was then the Australian colony of Victoria. His father William, who was successively a goldfield magistrate, judge and barrister, was a strict parent and a firm believer in discipline. Once issuing a proclamation to the Chinese gold miners under his wardship: 'W. H. Gaunt, your protector – tremble and obey.' In contrast, Ernest's mother Elizabeth was a 'delightfully vague' free spirit.

Ernest grew up in Ballarat – one of the wealthiest of the gold rush towns – where his family lived on the edge of town beside the Dark Swamp. There he, his four brothers and two sisters enjoyed the freedom and adventure of playing in the bush. His younger brother Guy remembered: 'life was full of incident for us. We had as many ponies as we wished to ride, the excitement of cattle-mustering and orchards full of gaily plumaged parrots … we could shoot possums and flying squirrels.'

William and Elizabeth brought up their children in the Anglican religion instilling in them the values of fear of God, hard work, honesty and love of Queen and country. But despite the outward appearance of respectability and probity, family life was unsettled. William, who was fired from his judgeship, was a gambler who managed to alternatively win and lose large fortunes with the result that the family's finances were usually precarious. Whereas Elizabeth was an emotionally unstable alcoholic.

After a year at boarding school in Melbourne, the twelve year old Ernest was sent to England to enrol in the Royal Navy cadet school, *HMS Britannia* at Dartmouth. In those days, the navy felt it was essential to recruit and mould its future officers at a tender age. Therefore this slight and socially awkward boy found himself alone in the world and thousands of miles from home, but the navy became his calling and he went on to whole heartedly embrace his new life.

According to him: 'No other life can be compared to that of the Royal Navy; the traditions, the atmosphere, the necessary day and night ever-watchfulness and the aloofness set it apart from similarity with any other body of disciplined men'. And paraphrasing a pronouncement from the reign of Charles II he liked to say, that it was the navy 'on which, under the good Providence of God, that the wealth, strength and safety of the Empire chiefly depend'.

Though of average academic ability, with determination and hard work, he steadily moved up the ranks, becoming a skilled and accomplished sailor with an aptitude for leadership. Admiral Seymour wrote: 'he is zealous, diligent and has much sound common sense and good judgement. A reliable man.'

By the late 1890s, he was a lieutenant stationed in China when he fell in love with an Irish beauty Louise Geraldine Martyn (or 'Gerry' as she was known to her friends). Louise was from an old Anglo-Norman Catholic family and grew up at Gregans Castle in the remote and beautiful Burren of County Clare. But even though her family were well respected, they were of modest means – just like the Gaunts – and she had travelled to Hong Kong seeking a husband. She was part of what was known as 'the fishing fleet' – an annual migration of young ladies from Britain to the colonies in search of an eligible bachelor. And Ernest fitted the description.

Gaunt was smitten and was intent on marrying her; though when proposing he explained that the navy would always come first, she second and any children third. Somehow this was insufficient to deter Louise. However there was one final hiccup when she insisted on getting married in a Catholic church and on raising their children in her religion, to which a furious Gaunt reacted by almost 'sending his bride back to her [Irish] bog.' But he relented and the wedding went ahead in 1899 in Hong Kong.

Ernest and Louise were a study in contrasts. He was self-controlled, disciplined, logical and at times given to a brooding depression. She was passionate, charismatic, volatile and vain. He was a sober Protestant; she was a devout Catholic who believed in saints and miracles. Though tempestuous at times, it proved to be a long and successful marriage and the couple went on to have three children: John, Sheila and Yvonne.

Louise frequently accompanied her husband as he moved from station to station – partially because she enjoyed the prestige of being an officer's wife and in part to prevent him from straying.

In China Ernest, though having no legal training, spent a stint as a colonial judge, where he acquired a reputation for 'simple and swift justice' and later in Constantinople he distinguished himself with his astute diplomacy.

But it was Ernest's command of *HMS Cambrian* that proved his mettle. In October 1905 having provisioned the ship at Queenstown he and his crew of 315 sailed out of Cork bound for Australia. Among the supplies and equipment on board were four trusty Maxim guns.

For the next two years, Gaunt embarked on a series of marathon voyages. From Cork, he sailed to Sydney by way of the Suez Canal and the Indian Ocean. From Australia, he traversed the Pacific stopping off in New Zealand, Honolulu and onto Acapulco, Mexico. Then he voyaged down the west coast of Latin America until he reached Chile, along the way meeting with the presidents of Honduras, Guatemala, Panama and Nicaragua. When he hosted President Zelaya of Nicaragua for lunch, the president even brought on board his fifty-four member band. As always Gaunt saw things from a colonial perspective and in Colombia he was struck by the 'sloth and indolence' of the locals. After Chile, he visited some of the most isolated islands in the world – Easter Island, Pitcairn and Tahiti – before returning to base at Sydney.

In 1907, the *Cambrian* left on a four month patrol of Melanesia. There had recently been outbreaks of violence in the two island groups of the New Hebrides and the Solomon Islands with missionaries and traders being attacked in retaliation for the behaviour of European settlers and the aggressive policies of the Australian authorities. Whereas in Latin America Ernest was entrusted with 'showing the flag' – demonstrating the power and reach of the Royal Navy – on his voyage to Melanesia his role was to enforce law and order according to English dictates and norms.

Whenever he received reports of unrest Gaunt sent parties ashore, armed with rifles and a Maxim gun, to attack and burn villages and crops. He was however frustrated that the locals would not fight according to British rules, complaining: 'The natives are arrant cowards, the thick bush enables them to fire rifles from within a few feet of a man, while they themselves are unseen by him, and they will

31

'snipe' a small party when they will not venture to attack a large one.' And after several patrols were ambushed in the New Hebrides, resulting in the death of one of his sailors, he abandoned the tactic.

When he moved on to Malaita in the Solomons – home to 'cannibals of the most depraved sort' – he resorted to bombarding the villages from the safety of the *Cambrian*. In the process causing considerable destruction such that the missionary Florence Young later 'found the natives to be in a state of terror'.

However, these attacks were of dubious value. The *Sydney Morning Herald* dismissed them as 'absolutely useless' and the Australian paper the *Sunday Times* rebuked Gaunt in a satirical poem:

> Let other nations belittle or scoff,
> The Boss picked the Briton to manage the show.
> With banner and bottle – with Bible and drum,
> With bullet and powder and fire and sword,
> With clashing of steel and the leaden rain's hum,
> With blood and with ruin he fights for the Lord!
> But it's only for civilization.

Returning to Australia after the Solomons Gaunt's tour of duty was finally over. In all he had sailed 103,000 kilometres – two and a half times the earth's circumference – in one of the epic voyages of the Edwardian era, leading the *Manchester Courier* to write that the achievement was 'without parallel' in modern naval history. He had accomplished this without ever running aground or endangering his ship, while sailing poorly charted and treacherous seas; he was without doubt a first rate captain.

Gaunt was awarded the navy's most prestigious command – captaincy of a mighty battleship – and in quick succession, he captained *HMS Majestic*, *Queen* and *Superb*. In 1913, he was appointed naval aide-de-camp to King George V, who took a deep interest in the navy and the pair developed a warm rapport. Thereafter Gaunt became a regular visitor to Buckingham Palace.

In the summer of 1914 with the outbreak of the First World War Ernest was overjoyed to be promoted to rear-admiral and assigned to the Grand Fleet based in Scotland. The fleet, comprising twenty-two battleships and fourteen swift battle-cruisers, was the greatest naval force ever assembled and was led by his old friend and mentor Admiral John Jellicoe. Jellicoe embodied all the traits that Ernest most admired – thoroughly professional, iron self-control and possessing a sharp and analytical mind. He was a moderniser but also a staunch believer in the navy's traditions. Ernest regarded him as the greatest admiral ever, 'far superior to Nelson, Drake and all the others.'

Jellicoe's arch nemesis was Admiral David Beatty commander of the fleet's battle-cruisers. Beatty was smart, impetuous, nonchalant and flamboyant. But he was politically astute and he aligned himself with another disrupter, Winston Churchill. Gaunt 'worshipped' Jellicoe, but he 'loathed' Beatty and Churchill.

For most of the war the Grand Fleet kept the Germans confined to their North Sea base at Wilhelmshaven. However, on 31 May 1916 Admiral Richard Scheer decided to break out. On learning that Scheer had mobilised, Jellicoe sailed south to engage him off the coast of Jutland. And as the two fleets bore down on each other Gaunt was on the bridge of his flagship *HMS Colossus* in command of a division of four powerful dreadnoughts. With great skill, Jellicoe deployed his warships into a single line ready to broadside the approaching enemy; it looked like it was going to be a turkey shoot.

But further to the south Beatty attacked the German fleet first and after a mauling, withdrew to the north, in the process interposing his battle cruisers between Jellicoe's battleships and the approaching Germans. With the battleships about to open fire, Beatty's arrival threw the whole scene into confusion. An infuriated Gaunt complained: '[my] division was unable to open fire upon the enemy owing to the battle cruisers being in between, and when they cleared from the battleships it made it extremely difficult to ascertain whether ships coming into view through the mist were friend or foe.' Nevertheless, the Grand Fleet subjected the Germans to a ferocious bombardment.

At his command post in the *Colossus'* citadel Gaunt was in the epicentre of the fight. With the air thick with smoke and the smell of cordite, he coolly endured the deafening roar of the guns and the shuddering of the thick steel plates from the impact of shells and shrapnel. Dudley Pound, his flag captain, reported the '*Colossus* passed through a cloud of fire, spray and smoke and they [the rest of the division] thought we were done for.' Another officer reported: 'things became very lively'.

Two shells fired by the battle cruiser *Seydlitz* hit the *Colossus*, one of which failed to explode. The other went right through the ship and exploded on the port side, where it destroyed a four inch gun and ignited boxes of cordite starting a fire. Three marines at an adjacent gun were injured as were two of Gaunt's domestics who were by his cabin rather that at their stations. In all the *Colossus* fired ninety-three massive rounds – each weighing almost 400 kilograms – from its twelve inch guns.

Finally, at nightfall the Germans escaped back to the safety of Wilhelmshaven, where they remained for the remainder of the war, with the Royal Navy retaining command of the sea.

The British press acclaimed Beatty as the hero of the battle, whereas Jellicoe was portrayed as indecisive and overly cautious. Before the year was out Beatty replaced him as commander of the Grand Fleet and in 1919 he was appointed First Sea Lord or professional head of the navy. Gaunt was furious with the trashing of Jellicoe and the lionisation of Beatty: 'that fool Beatty for taking his battle-cruisers between the enemy and the Grand Fleet'. He complained bitterly to Sir Edmund Barton, the former prime minister of Australia: 'We are up against such a nation of liars that it is doubtful whether the truth will win out, but I think we gave the Huns a thorough hammering.'

However, Gaunt received wide recognition and the following year he was appointed navy commander-in-chief of the East Indies. In 1919, Ernest was promoted to vice admiral and the next year he was knighted.

In December 1919, Admiral Sir Ernest and Lady Gaunt

returned to London where they thrived in their new found status. They were invited to receptions at the palace and the *Times* even reported on their annual holidays to the south of France. At official functions, he looked splendid in his dress uniform, with admiral's gold stripes on the sleeves, gold epaulettes, a chestful of medals and a ceremonial sword at his waist.

But Ernest and Louise were also insecure and acutely aware of their outsider status. They were poorly educated and had no wealth beyond his relatively modest salary. He was a 'colonial'- looked down upon by English-born snobs – and descended from impoverished minor gentry from Staffordshire. All of which encouraged the family to promote the fiction that they were ancestors of John of Gaunt (1340–1399), son of Edward III, and therefore of royal lineage. While Louise, embellished her family's story saying at various times that they owned a large brewery or that she was the daughter of Sir Nicolas O'Conor, from County Roscommon, a prominent British diplomat of the Victorian era. But there was no denying that Ernest's career was on a great trajectory; after all his predecessor in the East Indies Admiral Rosslyn Wemyss went on to be appointed First Sea Lord.

The Great War was over and with Britain teetering on the edge of bankruptcy, the government planned to drasti- cally downsize the navy and retire many of its officers. Still Ernest had good reason to be optimistic and he aspired to be appointed a governor of one of the Australian states. He had spent years lobbying for the position and had built up an influential network of supporters both in Australia and

England. A governorship would be a wonderful ending to his career, carrying with it enormous prestige and social standing which both he and Gerry would thoroughly enjoy. There is little better in life than to be welcomed home a hero.

However, Ernest was still stewing over Beatty's conduct at Jutland and in the navy's report published in 1920, his criticisms became public; the newspapers reported his comment that Beatty's behaviour had been 'unfortunate'. This was the first time he ever made such a foolish indiscretion.

Eventually in late 1920, Ernest was summoned to Whitehall to meet with Prime Minister Lloyd George and Walter Long, First Lord of the Admiralty (the cabinet minister in charge of the navy). It's almost certain that Beatty, as the First Sea Lord, was there also. Both the prime minister and Long told Gaunt that they had decided to appoint him commander of the Royal Navy in Ireland. He was the ideal person for the job.

Britain's hold on Ireland was slipping and the country was becoming ungovernable. Gaunt however had all the skills needed for the position. Throughout his career, he had shown himself to be a resourceful leader and an accomplished diplomat. He was unflappable and deliberate; never known to make a rash decision. Plus the fact that his wife was a Catholic might assuage Irish nationalists.

Gaunt resisted the idea. He regarded the Irish as 'impossible' – not least from his experiences with his own wife – and he knew that a posting in Ireland was the graveyard of many a career. But his superiors were insistent. Long promised, or at least intimated, that on completion of the two year assignment he would get the governorship that he so coveted. And so with much misgiving he relented. It's impossible to know what Beatty thought of the whole episode, but maybe he was happy to see Gaunt set up for a fall.

In his imperial hubris, Ernest had no sympathy for the Irish separatists and regarded the IRA as a bunch of mindless assassins. Throughout his career, he had effortlessly dealt with colonial unrest, and whereas the Irish might prove a thornier problem, he gave them no credit for possessing any military prowess. Like his father before him, he would protect the law abiding and compel murders and thugs to tremble and obey.

3

A RUTHLESS BASTARD

If you were to travel west along the main Cork to Kerry road during the War of Independence, having left the relative safety of Macroom – forty kilometres from Cork city – you entered bandit country. This was the mountainous terrain of west Cork where the IRA roamed freely; it was where they hid out, recuperated, trained and staged numerous ambushes. In the words of Charles Browne a local IRA volunteer: it 'was unpoliced and unwatched by the enemy.' Even the regular RIC had to be evacuated and only heavily armed convoys of Auxiliaries and soldiers dared enter. In early 1921 Seán O'Hegarty set up headquarters in the locality

Macroom was one of the most heavily policed towns in Ireland. It was the main base in Cork for the Auxiliaries – who were billeted in the castle on market square – and soldiers of the feared Essex Regiment patrolled in strength.

To maintain a token presence in the countryside once or twice a week a force of Auxiliaries left Macroom and drove out along the Kerry road. They always departed just after nine o'clock in the morning and travelled in a fleet of lorries, cars and the occasional armoured car, often bringing along hostages in the hope that they'd deter an ambush.

Twelve kilometres beyond Macroom, they passed through the townland of Coolnacaheragh (pronounced Cool-na-ca-her-ra), where there was a broad U-shaped bend in the road. The road curved around a steep hill, strewn with large boulders and to the south there was a smaller hill in the centre overlooking a ditch that ran alongside the road to the east. In the distance, mountains surrounded the scene to the north, south and west. This was where Seán O'Hegarty decided to stage an ambush in February 1921.

He and his deputy Dan 'Sandow' O'Donovan, planned meticulously; they didn't know when the Auxies would come, but they knew that eventually they would. They assembled a formidable force about sixty strong, armed with fifty-six rifles, two Lewis machine guns, ten shotguns and a stockpile of hand grenades. The nucleus of the unit was the brigade's flying column under the command of Sandow, which was supported by columns from Ballyvourney and Macroom.

O'Hegarty set up his command post on the steep hill close to the centre of the bend. The brigade's flying column, along with the Ballyvourney column, was deployed in a line stretching east to west for hundreds of metres along the hill and overlooking the road. At both ends was a machine gun nest. The Macroom column was mainly positioned on the small hill to the south of the road, with a clear view of the ditch further to the east where the Auxiliaries were expected to take cover having dismounted from their vehicles. At the far end of the ditch, there were two labourers' cottages.

On the eastern side, before the bend, there was a side-road which bypassed the ambush site and O'Hegarty had this trenched and assigned a party armed with shotguns to guard it. At the western end, he concealed a farm cart which could be quickly pulled across the road if the Auxies broke through

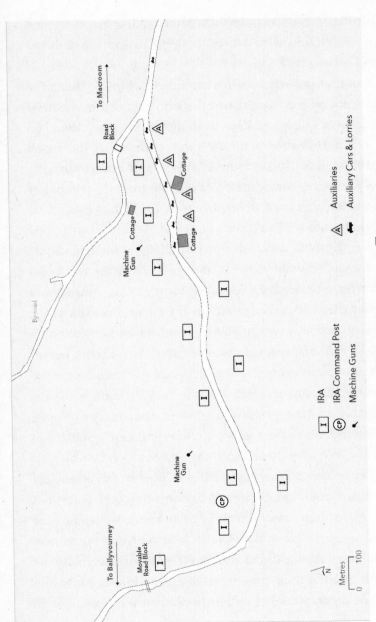

To Macroom

Road Block

Cottage

Cottage

Machine Gun

Cottage

By-road

Machine Gun

CP

To Ballyvourney

Movable Road Block

Auxiliaries

Auxiliary Cars & Lorries

IRA

IRA Command Post

Machine Guns

N

Metres
0   100

The Coolnacaheragh Ambush, 25 February 1921

41

the ambush. Scouts equipped with signalling flags occupied the high ground with orders to alert O'Hegarty when the patrol was sighted.

On four non-consecutive mornings before daybreak the men were roused from their billets in scattered farmhouses and after a quick breakfast and cup of tea, they marched close to ten kilometres in the pitch dark across the rough terrain to Coolnacaheragh. It was tough going; carrying rifles and heavy packs, their feet soaking from the wet boggy ground and at any moment they were liable to stumble over a rock or onto a gorse bush.

For three full days, the fighters took up position, concealing themselves behind the boulders. The weather was awful and in the morning there was frost on the ground. Throughout the day they had no hot food; lunch consisted of a thick slice of bacon between two chunks of bread washed down with a mug of cold tea, smoking was not allowed and they had to content themselves with chewing tobacco or sucking sweets. The normally sanguine Sandow complained: 'Jesus, but it was miserable, moving into position before dawn every morning, staying there in the wet and cold all day and moving out again at night. We were drenched to the skin most of the time.'

With such a large force lying in wait it was inevitable that word would get back to Macroom. But O'Hegarty told Sandow 'it didn't matter if the British knew, we would take on as many Auxies as they had in Macroom and beat them. I said no more, one didn't argue too much with Seán.' By the fourth day the men were worn out, morale was collapsing and the scouts were late in getting to their positions.

Finally, that morning at 7:30 – an hour and a half earlier than usual – the Auxies left Macroom with a significantly increased strength of seventy officers. They were dressed in their distinctive outfit of an army great coat, Scottish tam o'shanter cap and leather ammunition bandoliers slung like a sash over their chests. Except for their commanders, everyone carried a Lee-Enfield rifle and a brace of .45 Webley revolvers, many also had a bunch of hand grenades. Boxes of reserve ammunition were loaded onto the lorries and then they set off; they were armed to the teeth, trained to the hilt and equipped with thousands more rounds than O'Hegarty and his fighters.

Their commander Maj. Seafield-Grant travelled in the lead vehicle, a Ford touring car, and behind him came two more Fords and five Crossley tenders. The Crossley was a light truck adapted to carry eleven officers; three in front and eight in the back sitting on benches and facing outwards. Though the lorries had twelve millimetre thick protective steel plates, the Auxiliaries sat high up and were exposed, so that in the event of coming under fire they had to jump out and seek cover at the side of the road. The convoy drove cautiously along the rutted, unpaved road, as the cadets scanned the surrounding farmland, rifles at the ready.

Without any warning from the IRA scouts, the patrol rounded the corner into the bend, catching the ambush party completely off guard. The leading Ford came to a sudden stop when an officer saw a volunteer scrambling up the hill and moving from rock to rock. As soon as O'Hegarty realised that the Auxies weren't going to drive all the way into the ambush he gave the order to open fire. However, his force was in considerable disarray and Sandow was stuck near the road, from where it took him thirty minutes to get back to the command post.

After Maj. Grant, who had dismounted and was standing in the middle of the road, was killed in the opening volley, most of the Auxies retreated and barricaded themselves into the two cottages on the south side. The IRA began to strafe the cottages, though there was still confusion on the hill, with some of the men thinking that a withdrawal had been ordered. The disorder was compounded by the actions of Patrick 'Cruxy' O'Connor – an ex-British soldier in charge of the Lewis machine gun on the eastern side – who having fired a single burst ran off and abandoned his gun, later claiming it had jammed.

O'Hegarty and Sandow reasserted control and pressed the attack on the cottages. With bullets whizzing in through the doors and windows the Auxies were trapped and were unable to break cover to fire back. They desperately punched holes in the walls to make improvised loopholes for their rifles, but the attackers were able to rake the openings. Eugene O'Sullivan – another ex-soldier – the machine gunner on the western flank crept closer to the cottages and skilfully let loose short bursts through the cottage doors. The firing from the westernmost cottage began to slacken and the situation looked dire for the cornered Auxies.

In the meantime the Crossley tender in the rear of the convoy managed to reverse back down the road, turn around and return to Macroom and two hours after the fighting began a strong relief force of soldiers arrived in lorries. This time the scouts signalled and Seán O'Hegarty fired his semi-automatic Mauser into the air to order the retreat. Then as the Macroom column fought off an attempt by the Auxiliaries to outflank them, the entire ambush party withdrew to the north-west in the direction of the Kerry border. That evening O'Hegarty again successfully fought off an attempt by soldiers of the Royal Fusiliers to surround him.

In all three Auxiliaries were killed, including Maj. Grant, and eight were wounded, while there wasn't a single IRA casualty. O'Hegarty made a number of errors, the most crucial of which were not having his scouts in place and of wearing out his force by failing to understand that few possessed his endurance and stamina. It was beyond his control that Cruxy O'Connor – who was afterwards exposed as a traitor – abandoned his Lewis gun and this loss was likely a significant factor in the Auxies' survival. But on the other hand, Seán demonstrated consummate skill in planning and staging the ambush and in successfully extricating his force.

Paradoxically Maj. Grant, an experienced officer and recipient of the Military Cross, made several major blunders and failed to adhere to standard military procedure. He should not have sat exposed in the lead car, nor should he have stood in the middle of the road without taking cover. He failed to space his vehicles sufficiently apart so as to prevent most of them driving too far forward and getting trapped in the crossfire. He drove head long into the ambush without having guards crossing the fields on foot on either side of the road ready to encircle the ambushers. O'Hegarty himself knew well the importance of flanking guards and they had saved his life on at least one occasion.

Predictably the army refused to accept that a mere sixty fighters could pose such a threat and asserted that 'the strength of the column was considerably greater' with the *Daily Mail* reporting that there were 'four hundred rebels'. The truth however was humiliating; an attack led by a clerk and a carpenter threatened to overrun a heavily armed force, all of whom were ex-army officers and veterans of the First World War.

The British knew that O'Hegarty had come tantalising close to victory and thereafter the Auxiliaries largely avoided the area.

Seán O'Hegarty, who had been a revolutionary since his youth, possessed the mindset of a nineteenth century Fenian, but his methods were decidedly twentieth century. For him England was 'the greatest marauder in the world … [Ireland's] ancient, unchangeable and implacable enemy' and the sole aim of the IRA was 'to break the connection with England and establish an Irish Republic'.

He was entirely unremarkable in appearance; small in stature, with unhealthy sallow skin, thinning hair, a heavy black moustache and bat ears and dressed in a cheap suit. In 1921 at the age of forty, he was already ten to twenty years older than the rest of his officers and men.

But there was a 'determination that literally blazed in his eyes'. He was fearless, ruthless and possessed a 'rapier like intelligence'. Known for his 'lashing tongue' and 'sharp and sarcastic wit', his subordinates – with a heavy dose of wry Cork wit – referred to him as the 'Joker', though at other times he was simply called 'the chief'. And although his brigade had some of the toughest fighters in the IRA, he 'ruled the roost with an iron hand'. He was an abrasive and fiercely proud Cork city man.

He was a strict disciplinarian – a non-smoker and non-drinker – who abhorred drunkenness. Impervious to his own suffering and deprivation he shared in all the dangers and hardships; whether it was crossing a mountain path in the dead of night with snow on the ground or walking past an army patrol on the streets of Cork with a revolver in his pocket. Most of his subordinates were in awe of him and those who were closest saw at times an almost fatherly figure – though he hid his emotions behind a gruff facade of sour and uncomplimentary remarks. Florence O'Donoghue, his intelligence officer, remarked: 'any of us would have gladly put our bodies between him and a bullet'.

He had no desire for glory or public adulation and unlike many of the IRA's other leaders he was never photographed in a fine army officer's uniform. He once evaded a major British roundup in west Cork disguised as a scruffy tramp – mutton chop side whiskers, a tattered bowler hat and ragged patched coat and trousers, without a collar and tie. His skin scratched and red from scabies because of living rough in barns and dugouts.

Seán was born in Cork city in 1881 in a little terraced house on Evergreen Street; his father John was a skilled plasterer and his mother Katherine stayed at home to care for

Seán and his older brother Patrick Sarsfield. However, when he was eight years old his father died of tuberculosis in the workhouse infirmary and the family was plunged into poverty. Katherine, pawned her wedding ring, and was forced to make a living washing clothes, scrubbing floors and cooking.

Through grit and perseverance, this remarkable woman provided a good home for her two sons, eventually sending them to the Christian Brothers' North Monastery school. On leaving school at the age of twelve Seán became a sorter at the post office.

When the Gaelic revival swept the country at the turn of the century Seán immersed himself in the study of the Irish language, he played the fiddle, captained the post office's hurling team and joined the Gaelic League and the Celtic Literary Society. But above all he was committed to an independent Ireland and in 1906, on the recommendation of his brother who was a member of the Supreme Council of the Irish Republican Brotherhood (IRB), he was appointed head of the organisation in the city.

In December 1913 he became a founding member of the Irish Volunteers in Cork and though the organisation was ostensibly set up to advance the cause of Home Rule, O'Hegarty and his comrades in the IRB surreptitiously used it as an instrument for revolution. The following year with the outbreak of First World War, the authorities singled him out as a dangerous subversive and having refused a transfer to England, he was fired from the post office and forced to leave Cork city. And it was when he was in west Cork working as a farm labourer that he learned of the 1916

Easter Rising in Dublin and the failure of the volunteers in Cork to join in the fight. This humiliation haunted him for the rest of his life.

During the Great War he stockpiled explosives and wrote leaflets urging people to welcome the German army as liberators: 'When the Germans come they will come as friends, to put an end to English rule in Ireland.'

In 1917, Seán returned to the city where he applied for the position of storekeeper at the workhouse. This was a political appointment – controlled by the Ancient Order of Hibernians – and the holder was expected to enrich himself and his supporters at the expense of the inmates. When eight other candidates dropped out O'Hegarty got the job. It was believed that he and the IRB had intimidated the other applicants and a subsequent inquiry cautiously concluded: 'upon careful consideration of the evidence they [the investigators] are of the opinion that while the methods adopted for securing the election of Mr. Hegarty appear to have been of doubtful propriety' the allegations remained unproven.

With his characteristic fervour and profound sense of justice he tackled the endemic corruption – against the wishes of the workhouse's Board of Guardians – by bringing to public attention issues such as the reselling of bread and flour and the purchase of substandard clothing and milk and his efforts led to a big improvement in conditions. It's said that on one occasion having been offered a bribe he threw the transgressor down the stairs. One has to wonder whether his father's fate in the workhouse was a motivating factor in his zeal.

By then Seán was married to Maghdalen (Míd) Ní

Laoghaire, an ardent Gaelic Leaguer and president of Cumann na mBan (the Women's Council, a paramilitary republican organisation) in Cork. During the war, she duped the British government into funding first aid and nursing classes for her members, on the pretext that they were planning to care for wounded soldiers. Subsequently in 1917 she was imprisoned for collecting donations for Irish political prisoners and after a brief hunger strike, resulting in considerable embarrassment to the government, she was released.

Courageous and outspoken, Míd shared Seán's obstinacy leading to tensions within Cumann na mBan, which erupted out into the open after she organised a fund raising *céilí* (dance) on Saint Patrick's Day which also happened to be Palm Sunday eve. This was too much for her more religious colleagues who ousted her from the leadership. During the War of Independence, it was said that she ran a café in the city centre, which was a meeting point for the IRA.

When the Volunteers reorganised in the aftermath of the Rising Seán was appointed vice-commander of the Cork brigade, under Tomás MacCurtain, who was also Cork's Sinn Féin Lord Mayor. In contrast to MacCurtain's cautious approach, Seán was determined to provoke an all-out war and he gathered around himself a faction referred to as 'Hegarty's crowd' whom he inducted into the IRB. The group, including Sandow O'Donovan, Mick Murphy and Tom Crofts, constituted a secret clique within the brigade and was responsible for the majority of bombings and shootings in the city over the subsequent few years.

In September 1917, they carried out their first significant operation when they raided the armoury of the officer training corps at Cork Grammar School, hauling away forty-seven rifles and two revolvers. From then on there was a steady escalation of activity. The next year they staged a daring rescue of one of their own, Donnchadha MacNeilus from Cork Jail with the rescuers posing as visitors including one who was disguised as a priest. Gun attacks on the police commenced towards the end of 1919 and by 1920 things really started to heat up.

The RIC stopped patrolling the streets, until the Black and Tans and the Auxiliaries reinforced them later in 1920. In March alone two police were killed and a number of others injured, leading MacCurtain to condemn O'Hegarty and his crowd: 'We can't have men roaming around armed shooting police on their own.' That evening a police death squad murdered MacCurtain. He was succeeded by Terence MacSwiney, a poet and dreamer, who was in turn arrested by the army in August and died later that year on hunger strike in Brixton Prison in England.

With Seán now the 'unchallenged leader' of Cork No. 1 Brigade – responsible for the city and surrounding countryside – attacks against the police and army continued unabated. In December alone five police officers were killed. The following month Mick Murphy – who commanded the IRA's second battalion with responsibility for the southern half of Cork city – attacked an RIC patrol in broad daylight in the city centre, killing two constables and injuring four. To the consternation of the police this was the first time the IRA used a Lewis machine gun in the city.

By this time, the city resembled a war zone. City Hall and much of the centre had been burnt to the ground, when drunken Auxies went on a rampage in December. Soldiers and Auxiliaries charged through the city streets in lorries and armoured cars, setting up checkpoints and cordoning off areas to conduct sweeps. Armed sentries and patrols were everywhere and at night they enforced a curfew. The court house on Washington Street was protected by soldiers in steel helmets, armed with rifles and machines guns and behind a wall of sandbags fronted by barbed wire. The army at Victoria Barracks even had its own tank formation.

By January, O'Hegarty decided that to effectively lead the brigade he needed to move his headquarters out of the city to the Ballyvourney area.

Seán (and not without reason) was obsessed with the threat posed by spies and informers and he carried out far more executions than any other brigade commander. At least twenty-seven suspected informers were executed in the city alone, not counting killings in the brigade area outside of the city and many unexplained 'disappearances'. The latter being his preferred modus operandi.

Cork No. 1 operated two secret prisons, the most notorious of which – known as Sing Sing – was in Knockraha in east Cork, and consisted of a half-submerged, soundproof crypt in a graveyard. The prisoners were taken out of their cell at night to be shot and secretly buried in a field. Mick Leahy, the brigade's vice-commander, claimed that '90 spies are buried near Knockraha'. According to the chief jailer and executioner, Martin Corry: 'Seán O'Hegarty was a great man. He never asked awkward questions'

Ernie O'Malley, a senior IRA officer, remarked that O'Hegarty 'had the name of not being very particular about evidence.' Florence O'Donoghue once presented him with arguments both for and against the guilt of a suspect, until O'Hegarty exploded: 'kill the bastard – what good is he anyway'.

In February 1921 Seán O'Hegarty, authorised the killing of an elderly widow Maria Lindsay, a friend of Gen. Peter Strickland, the army commander in Cork. Mrs Lindsay gave information to the RIC resulting in the capture and execution of five volunteers and in retaliation she was kidnapped by Frank Busteed, who said he shot 'that old bitch' after O'Hegarty gave him the go ahead. O'Hegarty acted without getting permission from Michael Collins and IRA headquarters (GHQ) and the brutality of the episode left a lingering bitterness between him and the Dublin leadership.

Irrespective of the morality of his methods, the policy had a chilling effect and Gen. Crozier, the commander of the Auxiliaries, admitted that 'it was madness to inform'.

Seán was an intensely private person, who rarely socialised outside of nationalist and IRA circles. He didn't leave any personal papers and he and Míd didn't have children, who could have told their story. Aside from references to his abrasive personality, intelligence, caustic sense of humour and bravery there is very little mention of his inner or personal life. He had no interest in personal wealth or public recognition.

One of his few indulgences was chatting over cups of tea with his comrades. His political views were uncomplicated and unyielding, though he was also a pragmatist. In everything he did, he was as straight and as deadly as an arrow.

He was tough, so tough that even Sandow O'Donovan said of him: 'he was a ruthless bastard'. As Yeats wrote in his poem *Easter, 1916*: 'Too long a sacrifice can make a stone of the heart'.

4

BUGGER ALL

Having spoken to an ex-British soldier, Patrick O'Sullivan, the captain of the IRA company in Ballyvourney, came away with a brilliant idea. He was convinced that equipped with a 'miracle weapon' he'd blow the local RIC barracks to smithereens and then moving the weapon around Cork, he'd destroy barracks after barracks. There'd be no stopping him and the lads from Ballyvourney.

And so one evening in 1919 he assembled thirty fighters armed with shotguns and revolvers along with two farm carts – one pulled by a horse and the other by a stubborn donkey – piled high with ropes, wooden planks and long thick poles. At eight o'clock they left Ballyvourney, travelling along the by-roads to avoid detection; they trudged on for sixteen kilometres; up and down hills and valleys, desperately trying to prevent an axle breaking on one of the innumerable pot holes and deep ruts.

They marched as quietly as possible, constantly on the look out, not just for the police but also for the Macroom IRA into whose territory they were trespassing. IRA areas were sacrosanct and this unauthorised intrusion was a grievous insult. Four or five hours later the road started to gently descend and they passed the two-storey terrace houses on the outskirts of Macroom, they crossed the old nine-arched stone bridge over the River Sullane, went up the steep hill into the centre of town and made a sharp right turn into market square. There they came face to face with their prey.

Two rusty cannons in front of the gates of Macroom castle. They were massive pieces of cast iron embossed with the arms of George III (1738–1820) and resting on equally immense metal gun carriages. They must have weighted at least 2,000 kilograms. O'Sullivan's plan was that they'd haul the cannons back to Ballyvourney, pack them with gunpowder, ram in a one kilogram iron ball – of the sort used for the Cork sport of road bowling – and blast the walls and doors of the RIC barracks. After which he and his men would rush in, capture the stunned police and carry off their weapons.

It was early morning and the town was fast asleep with only the occasional barking dog interrupting the silence. Fortunately, the Auxiliaries had not yet moved into the castle, though there was still the risk of discovery by an RIC or army patrol. Quietly and efficiently, they went to work.

Using the planks, they made a ramp at the back of each cart and then attached the ropes to the guns. Half the group pulled on the ropes, while the rest used the poles to lever the guns up the ramps. They were strong country lads and they pulled and heaved with all their might, but the cannons never so much as budged. Finally, close to daybreak, Pat O'Sullivan was forced to call off the operation and he and his dejected fighters marched wearily back home.

But O'Sullivan was not the only commander with a similar idea. Tom McEllistrim, a farmer and IRA captain in Kerry, led a group of 'powerful strong men' to Ross castle, the fifteenth century ancestral home of the O'Donoghues. Having inspected the ramparts, he selected three cannons. This time the IRA was successful. The largest gun was 'a fierce yoke' weighing one and a half tons (1,500 kilograms), which was loaded onto a sturdy wagon built to haul tree trunks.

At two in the morning, McEllistrim brought the guns through the streets of Killarney and hid them nearby. A blacksmith removed the spike in the touch holes and re-bore the barrels, which were clogged with centuries of rust and a metal worker made steel projectiles.

However, the cannons proved to be of more danger to their hapless handlers than to the RIC. The largest one 'smashed the cars on which it was loaded, lamed the horses that drew it, crushed fingers and toes. It slipped off a cart rolling madly downhill in erratic circles ... smashed through a gate and came to rest in a slimy ditch'. It was passed onto to Seán Moylan, the commander of the North Cork Brigade, who reported that when he test fired it there was a loud explosion; 'I was blinded with smoke ... My left hand was covered with blood and goblets of flesh hanging from it. That for me completed the day's experiment.' Fortunately, a local doctor, having given him a stiff whiskey for anaesthetic, patched him up

Eventually a pair of the guns saw action in the Civil War in July 1922 when the West Cork Brigade used them to seize Skibbereen from the pro-Treaty National Army. The smaller cannon was positioned in a bank 100 metres from the police station, and when it was fired there was an almighty explosion. 'Where's our gun?' asked one of the IRA. 'Where's my bank?'

inquired the bank manager. The bigger gun was then brought to within a few metres of the barracks, sandbags were placed around the wheels to absorb the recoil, a volunteer lit a fuse rather than risk directly lighting the touch hole and this time it successfully fired, blowing a hole in the barracks wall and forcing the shocked occupants to surrender.

Looking back a bloodied, but wiser Seán Moylan advised: 'Never put all your powder into one gun.'

Why did the IRA expend so much time and effort capturing and deploying eighteenth century cannons? Why did smart and experienced volunteers put so much faith in such a hare brained idea? Simply put, when it came to arms and ammunition the IRA had bugger all. In fact, it was truly remarkable that such an ill-equipped force was able to hold the mighty British army and the Auxiliary Division to a stalemate.

In May 1921 – when the IRA had approximately 2,000 active fighters – internal documents reported that its arsenal consisted of 569 rifles with twenty rounds per rifle, 477 revolvers and incongruously six swords and 220 pikes. Additionally there were hundreds of shotguns and a small quantity of machine guns.

Tom Barry wrote that the most the three Cork brigades ever had between them was 310 rifles and five machine guns, plus an assortment of revolvers and shotguns. But the main challenge was that 'ammunition did not exceed fifty rounds a rifle, two fills [approximately a dozen] per revolver and automatic and a few full drums [holding either forty-seven or ninety-seven rounds] for each machine gun'.

Seán O'Hegarty's plight was even greater than that of other commanders; given the strength of the British forces opposing him, the number of fighters he needed to arm and the fact that he had to conduct both urban and rural operations.

In the city, his guerrillas fought at close range with revolvers and hand grenades; appearing out of nowhere and then disappearing back into the crowd or into the night. Whereas in the countryside the shooting tended to be at a greater distance and to be more prolonged, requiring rifles, landmines and if possible machine guns. Rifles were necessary because their range and accuracy were considerably greater than that of either revolvers or shotguns.

Even when Seán led the unusually protracted ambush at Coolnacaheragh, his riflemen had at the most fifty rounds each and the two machine guns had only one or two pans of ammunition. While Daniel Corkery who led the Macroom column during the ambush reported his unit as being 'well armed', despite having a mere twenty rounds per rifle.

In general fifty rounds per fighter was considered good and given that the Lee Enfield rifle – the standard British army issue – could fire fifteen rounds per minute, this merely enabled a single volley lasting three or so minutes.

It was this extreme shortage of ammunition that proved even more significant than the lack of weaponry and explosives. Forcing O'Hegarty's columns to restrict themselves to short, sharp engagements.

During the brigade's attack on Blarney barracks, Leo Buckley, who was a member of a squad of eight tasked with preventing the British from bringing up reinforcements, reported: 'We had one Lee Enfield and an assortment of shotguns. At about 9 p.m. we heard the noise of a lorry coming towards our position. When it approached nearer, we found that there were two British Leyland lorries containing some ninety troops, obviously on their way to relieve Blarney police barracks. We waited until they were about 150 yards away, when we fired one round apiece. To our great surprise, we saw the officer and sergeant jump from the front seat of the first lorry and run back along the road, followed by the troops. We expected that they had taken up position to attack us, but it subsequently transpired that they ran all the way back to [Ballincollig] barracks.' Even allowing for some embellishment in the telling, Buckley and his comrades protected O'Hegarty's flank, despite their extremely limited weaponry. And there were numerous other successful engagements where the volunteers were just as poorly armed.

P. J. Murphy from Cork city stated: 'One was considered lucky if he had five [revolver] rounds going into action.' And in June 1921 the 1st Battalion, which was responsible for the northern half of the city, reported that it had less than ten bullets for each of its seventy revolvers. But remarkably, by that time the British had ceded control of much of Cork, with one of the leading guerrillas Patrick 'Pa' Murray stating: 'police patrols became less frequent, in fact they often did not appear on the streets for five or six days. We were patrolling the streets regularly … The movements of the British were restricted to travelling through the city area in lorries, protected by armoured cars.'

Cork No. 1 Brigade purchased, captured, manufactured and smuggled munitions, but it was never enough. Initially volunteers seized shotguns from farmers and 'big houses' and bribed soldiers home on leave to hand over their rifles. Peter O'Donovan, who was one of Hegarty's crowd, claims to have spent (the huge sum of) £300 from the brigade's funds buying guns from soldiers. P. J. Murphy was part of a group that took a bread van into Victoria Barracks in the middle of the day, bought a number of rifles, loaded them into the van and then drove back out through the main gate.

Soon the volunteers started attacking police and soldiers, stripping them of their arms. The level of violence progressively increased as the British became more prepared to repulse their attackers, until by the end of 1919 the IRA was forced to open fire first. Finally by 1920 the IRA was getting much of its munitions by storming RIC barracks and ambushing patrols.

But innovative and unorthodox tactics persisted. One volunteer, who was a medical student, stole 200 kilograms of lead for bullets from the roof of an allegedly haunted mansion. Though he failed in a subsequent attempt to seize a lead coffin from a crypt.

The brigade had considerable success in manufacturing explosives and bombs. Raymond Kennedy, a chemistry lecturer at the university, taught the volunteers how to make large quantities of guncotton (nitrocellulose) and detonators. Additionally they built electrically detonated mines, which though frequently unreliable, proved at times to be highly effective. At Youghal in May 1921, seven members of the Hampshire Regiment band were killed and twenty-one wounded by one concealed in a wall. And in east Cork clandestine workshops churned out thousands and thousands of high-quality hand grenades.

Seán O'Hegarty had a job for everybody. Seamus Fitzgerald, who was a Sinn Féin member of parliament, volunteered at the brigade's main bomb foundry in Knockraha. Henry O'Mahony, a fitter at Passage West dockyards in Cork Harbour, made cases for mines and bombs. Margaret Lucey of Cumann na mBan, who worked as a shorthand typist at Crosse & Blackwell foods, smuggled out empty tin cans to be used as bomb canisters.

However, Seán had little success with smuggling weapons. Most imported caches merely consisted of a few revolvers or a small quantity of ammunition brought in by ships' crew. Though in December 1920 he sent Mick Murphy to London where he bought two Lewis guns, along with revolvers and ammunition on the black market. The weapons were packed into barrels and sent by boat to the City of Cork Steam Packet's warehouse. On his return Murphy went to the warehouse where he had the barrels loaded onto a horse and cart and made his getaway. These were the Lewis guns used by the column at the Coolnacaheragh ambush.

By late 1920, Cork No. 1 was in dire straits; it was increasingly difficult to seize weapons and ammunition from the army and police, who rarely moved about except in considerable strength, while smuggling had achieved little to date.

Finally in December there was an unexpected development.

Michael Collins offered to arm the Cork brigades with a massive quantity of military grade arms and ammunition, far beyond what they had ever acquired before.

5

MICKY AND DICKY

Michael Collins is the towering figure of the War of Independence. He was 'the one man without whom the Irish revolution would probably not have succeeded.' He has been hailed as 'the man who made Ireland' and 'the founder of modern guerrilla warfare, the first freedom fighter'. Sometimes this hyperbole was contradictory as when his English biographer Rex Taylor wrote that while his subordinates considered him a God like 'supreme being' he was actually 'the very model of humanity'. The critical Peter Hart summed him up as 'the most ruthless, the most powerful, the most calculating and the most successful politician in modern Irish history.'

Collins was the IRA's *de facto* commander and the dominant figure at GHQ, which operated clandestinely out of offices and safe houses throughout Dublin. His comrades, who knew him as 'Mick', respected him for his intelligence, limitless energy, charisma and daring. He was decisive, possessed considerable administrative ability and his organisational skills were exceptional. He set up an intelligence service that largely eliminated the British spy network, while his presidency of the IRB consolidated his position as the most powerful person within the IRA.

Tom Barry said that 'without a shadow of a doubt ... [he

was] the effective driving force and the backbone at GHQ.' Adding that he was 'a tireless, ruthless, dominating man of great capacity, he worked like a Trojan in innumerable capacities to defeat the enemy.' Mick Leahy of Cork told the chief of staff Risteárd Mulcahy: 'Collins is GHQ and he owns your body and soul'. Peter Carleton of the Belfast IRA said: 'Collins had an aura that no one else had.'

Even the British held a grudging respect for him. Gen. Macready, the army commander in Ireland, was impressed by his ability to 'impose his will upon' his colleagues, finding him the 'easiest [of the Sinn Féiners] to deal with' and adding 'fearless he certainly was, to which he added a degree of cunning which stood him in good stead in many a tight corner.'

Whereas Mulcahy kept busy writing reports and issuing orders, Collins was the man of action. It was said that the only way to get anything done at GHQ was to 'see Mick'. James Malone, who worked directly for Collins, wrote approvingly: 'Mick didn't give a hoot about rules and regulations, so long as things were happening.'

Collins – in his capacity as the Minister of Finance in the Dáil cabinet led by Éamon de Valera – masterminded the raising of funds needed by both the government and the IRA. The money was raised in the form of Dáil Loans (or Republican Bonds), subscribed to by the public primarily in Ireland and the United States. His efforts were tremendously successful; £380,000 was raised in Ireland, and the Friends of Irish Freedom in America sent over $250,000, equivalent to a total considerably greater than €20,000,000 today.

Posterity has come to regard Collins as a financial genius and 'the general consensus ... [is that he] was the most effective member of the Dáil ministry.' Andrew McCarthy a historian at University College Cork, credits him as being 'outstanding' and of being 'Ireland's most distinguished' finance minister.

With all this money, Collins was in a strong position to smuggle large quantities of munitions. Since he also controlled a network of IRB operatives employed at British and Irish ports and he had his own arms purchasers on the continent. Moreover, in the aftermath of the Great War arms and ammunition were readily available on the European black market.

GHQ did import and sell military supplies to units throughout the country, but this was in small quantities and often at high prices. For example surviving records from the spring of 1920 show that over the course of five weeks Cork No. 1 was only able to purchase one parabellum and two .45 revolvers at £6 a piece. The same year Seán Moylan, who bought eight revolvers with ten rounds each, one rifle with fifty rounds and a dozen percussion bombs for £120, complained, 'I was paying through the nose for them'.

Collins organised one significant shipment to Seán O'Hegarty, when the German freighter *City of Dortmund* sailed into Cork with up to 200 semi-automatic Luger parabellums on board, which Seán had unloaded in potato sacks and driven away.

However, overall the results of Collins' efforts were dismal. Liam Lynch, the commander of the North Cork Brigade, which received only six or seven rifles from Dublin throughout the war, commented: '[GHQ] gave very little help to the country [brigades]'. Florence O'Donoghue stated GHQ supplied 'the minutest quantities' of arms. In Limerick Tomás Ó Maoileóin maintained that Collins 'starved' his brigade of weapons. Seán Culhane of Cork No. 1 complained that when he met Collins in Dublin he borrowed his two revolvers and never returned them as promised. The historian David Fitzpatrick wrote: 'GHQ obtained only six machine guns and about a hundred rifles in the year between August 1920 and July 1921', a period that covered the majority of the fighting of the War of Independence.

John Borgonovo aptly summed up this puzzling situation: 'considering the miniscule amount of money distributed to the country units and the failure of GHQ to import significant amounts of weapons, the question remains as to what happened to the millions raised in Ireland and overseas by the Republican movement. Though Collins' biographers depict him as a financial wizard, it seems remarkable that so little of the Minister of Finance's funds made their way into the hands of the IRA.'

Liam Mellows, who was the IRA's Director of Purchases and ostensibly in charge of arms procurement, believed that Michael Collins deliberately sabotaged and undermined his work. This was likely because Collins was well aware that controlling the importation and distribution of weapons helped him consolidate his power and influence. As Séumas [*sic*] Robinson, the commander of the South Tipperary Brigade and an ardent critic of Collins, put it: 'he liked to have a finger in the pie of every department.'

Collins' tactics left Seán O'Hegarty in a dilemma; if he depended on GHQ he was likely to receive hardly anything, whereas if he smuggled in weaponry himself he was subject to censure. After he sent Mick Murphy to London to buy weapons, Collins summoned Murphy to Dublin where 'he hauled me over the coals' accusing him of impeding the work of his own London IRB network. 'I bought two bloody machine guns for £20 and by God they'll be used by us Mick', replied Murphy. Collins, refusing to believe that Lewis guns could be bought so cheaply on the black market, meekly replied: 'Oh, be off out of that'.

Despite Collins' generally outstanding reputation, some of the provincial officers had their doubts. It was not lost on them that neither Collins nor any other senior officer at headquarters dared visit Cork during the entire war. Despite his bluster, Collins never participated in any of the fighting; in fact he had never fired a shot in battle. Séumas Robinson accused him of being an 'artful dodger' who 'was able to give the [false] impression to the Volunteer [IRA] officers from all over the country that he not only organised the attacks on spies [in Dublin] ... but that he also led them, taking part in them!'

It was Seán O'Hegarty, Tom Barry and other militants, and not Collins and GHQ, who were instrumental in escalating the conflict. In the words of David Fitzpatrick: 'headquarters followed helplessly some distance behind its more adventurous provincial followers.'

In April 1920 GHQ refused to give Cork No. 1 authorisation to attack RIC patrols throughout the city due to the risk of heavy casualties; a decision that resulted in considerable resentment among the Cork volunteers and pushed O'Hegarty to operate in the future without oversight. Though characteristically Collins later passed word on to O'Hegarty: 'it is always best to shoot first and ask permission afterwards'.

Collins conducted much of his business in pubs, knowing that this allowed a group of young men to come together without arousing suspicion. IRA officers from the country could contact him by visiting Devlin's in Parnell Street where he was to be seen most nights. Furthermore Collins liked to drink with subordinates, so that he could size them up and enlarge his network of allies. Tom Maguire, a senior officer from Mayo, had no time for Collins' 'bonhomie' and complained 'I did not like his habit of taking the country fellows off for a jar. He got a grip on fellows that way.'

But it wasn't all work and he loved to be in a pub surrounded by friends and comrades; a 'ball of malt' (glass of whiskey) in one hand and a cigarette in the other. He was a warm and generous host; witty and funny and 'a great swearer', though at times he became drunk and belligerent.

When Florence O'Donoghue went to Dublin in 1920 Collins took him and other officers out to a restaurant where to his surprise 'none of them appeared to be in imminent danger of arrest'. O'Donoghue was equally bemused that Risteárd Mulcahy was able to bring him back to the comfort of his home for lunch and introduce him to his wife. Liam Deasy had an even better time when he was summoned to

GHQ. Aside from several visits to Devlin's, Collins brought him to the horse-races at Phoenix Park and the following day to Lamb Doyle's Pub, in the foothills of the Dublin Mountains, for an afternoon of 'songs and stories'.

Despite being one of the most wanted fugitives in the country Collins' ability to move freely about Dublin – often brazenly passing through police and army checkpoints – was the stuff of legend; he was always 'one step ahead' of his would be captors. On one occasion Liam Deasy observed a plainclothes policeman seeming to recognise Collins in the street, but then simply walking away.

A typical close-call occurred when Collins brought a group out for dinner at the Gresham Hotel, one of the finest and most expensive hotels in the city, and where he later had a suite of rooms. The restaurant was raided by a patrol of Auxiliaries, specifically tasked with arresting him. The Auxies went straight to his table, one took a photograph out of his pocket, looked at it carefully and said 'You are Michael Collins'. Collins calmly replied 'No, I'm John Craig' and produced papers to back up his alibi, whereupon the Auxiliaries left and Collins and his friends proceeded to get drunk.

Florence O'Donoghue was not the only one puzzled by the authorities' inability to capture him. Mark Sturgis, a senior official at Dublin Castle, remarked: 'I wonder how it is that the Archbishop [Clune of Perth on a peace mission to Ireland] sees Collins apparently without difficulty in Dublin and our intelligence fails to find him after weeks of search.' J. B. Hittle, an expert on military intelligence, also questioned how he was able to remain free, despite 'concurrently exchanging communications' with Andy Cope, the Assistant Under-secretary at Dublin Castle. Gen. Macready blamed his 'hair-breath escapes' to be due in part 'to treachery or fear on the part of agents employed by the Crown'.

However, since late 1920 Collins was playing a double game. He was in contact with intermediaries attempting to reach a peace settlement and at the same time he needed continuing IRA violence to strengthen his hand in any negotiations. Outwardly he presented himself as 'an irreconcilable hardliner', but the British regarded him as someone they could make a deal with.

Therefore, Collins' ability to avoid arrest was likely due to a combination of factors: fear on the part of the police, his network of police informers, his security measures, quick thinking, good luck and especially that by early 1921 the leadership on both sides were increasingly desperate for peace. Michael Hopkinson wrote: 'later attempts to arrest him may at times have been less than whole-hearted'.

Seán O'Hegarty and Michael Collins had much in common; they were both smart, ruthless, fearless and domineering and they were both from Cork: Seán from the city and Mick from a small farm outside Clonakilty in the west. They were also Fenians to the core. But their differences were far more numerous. O'Hegarty who led an ascetic life was a teetotaller and a person of few words. He was above any suspicion of financial chicanery. He led and fought in numerous engagements and endured considerable hardship on the run. For him there were no merry evenings at the pub.

On the other hand, Collins was a flamboyant, boastful personality, a womaniser and drinker who relished the good life. Unlike O'Hegarty's brutal directness, Collins was duplicitous and skilled in the art of telling people what they wanted to hear. As J.J. Lee wrote: 'he clearly had the convenient knack of leaving different people with congenial but conflicting impressions of his real policy.' It was no wonder that Michael Leahy called Collins 'master of the revels' and Seán Moylan referred to O'Hegarty as 'master of invective'.

Leahy said of the pair: 'Collins and Seán O'Hegarty never liked each other. Seán H was certainly no diplomat. He was too abrupt, but he was thoroughly honest and thoroughly genuine.' The implication being that Collins was not 'thoroughly honest and thoroughly genuine'.

Accusations of financial impropriety were made against Collins as far back as 1917, though he and his allies mounted a fierce rebuttal, forcing his critics to back down. Later Cathal Brugha, the Sinn Féin Minister of Defence with whom he had an extremely fraught relationship, claimed that 'monies that Collins had the control of ... which were supposed to be used for the purchase of arms were being wasted or misspent or unlawfully made use of'.

By 1920, he was leading a lifestyle that was far beyond what he could have afforded had he remained a post office clerk. O'Hegarty heard about this carry on and he didn't like it one iota. It must have been obvious to him that Collins spent far more on drinks and entertainment than he spent on weapons for Cork.

Though if there was tension between Collins and O'Hegarty, the latter's relationship with the bureaucratic Mulcahy was even worse. On one occasion when Mulcahy criticised a failed attack on an RIC barracks, O'Hegarty wrote across the report, in big letters: 'Balls'. Not that Mulcahy thought any more highly of O'Hegarty, whom he referred to – with considerable justification – as 'always a snarly gob'. But the more astute and less sensitive Collins had a grudging respect for the irascible O'Hegarty.

O'Hegarty derisively referred to Collins and Mulcahy as 'Micky' and 'Dicky'; two out of touch arm-chair generals who sent him 'fanciful instructions' containing high-falutin' terms such as 'strategic necessity'. In a frustrated outburst, he told his comrades that he was sick of all the *raiméis* (rubbish) coming out of GHQ. He asked why hadn't Collins or Mulcahy inspected the southern brigades and seen for themselves the situation there? Why didn't they organise other areas of the country to fight and thereby relieve the pressure on the south? Why hadn't they imported the arms and ammunitions that were so badly needed?

However, Collins and O'Hegarty needed each other. If Collins was to get a peace settlement and an independent Ireland, it was imperative that the British be pushed to the negotiating table by the violence orchestrated by O'Hegarty and others like him. O'Hegarty, whose brigade was in dire risk of running out of bullets, knew that Collins was the only one with the resources to come to his assistance. It was no wonder that Collins warned de Valera: 'unless the boys get arms and ammunition it's all over.'

Meanwhile throughout the second half of 1920, Collins had been cultivating contacts with access to senior figures in the Italian government and by the end of the year there was a major breakthrough; the Italians were ready to commit to a massive shipment consisting of thousands of rifles and millions of rounds of ammunition. Seán O'Hegarty knew that this would be an absolute game changer.

Collins contacted the leadership in Cork and it was agreed that the cargo would be off loaded in Liam Deasy's territory of west Cork and Mick Leahy was chosen to travel to Italy to oversee the operation.

6

THE ITALIAN JOB

The twenty-five year old Mick Leahy was a qualified marine engineer and therefore one of the few IRA members capable of overseeing the operation. Originally from Queenstown, he had trained at the Royal Navy's Haulbowline dockyards and even though the town's RIC's district inspector warned that 'Leahy is still dangerous and should not be employed in the dockyards' the navy let him complete his apprenticeship.

Throughout the War of Independence Leahy demonstrated exceptional leadership and tactical skills, going on to become O'Hegarty's deputy. He established his reputation in January 1920 with the capture of the fortified RIC barracks in the village of Carrigtwohill. Even the normally reticent Risteárd Mulcahy was impressed and admitted that the engagement marked the escalation of the IRA's struggle into outright 'war'.

In early January 1921, Leahy took the train to Dublin to receive his orders. Heading to Wellington Quay he mounted the stairs to an office above Reliable Tailoring – 'offering exceptional value in suits of Irish material from forty-two shillings' – where he met Gearóid O'Sullivan, the IRA's adjutant-general.

Then according to Leahy:

> He set off with me and [we] made a very lengthy journey through many streets and eventually finished up at Devlin's public

house in Parnell Street, only the length of O'Connell Street [a few hundred metres] from where we started. I asked Gearóid why the considerable detour had been made and he said one couldn't be too careful in these times in Dublin on account of the likelihood of being followed by enemy touts. Nevertheless I had my suspicion that it was all done to impress me, the boy from the country. Actually when we entered Liam Devlin's pub I was surprised to find nearly all the GHQ staff assembled and a merry party in progress, this despite Gearóid's intimation that Dublin was a dangerous place for the likes of him.

My choice of lemonade when whiskey was being pressed on me did not go down too well with Michael Collins, who seemed to be the master of revels ... The party was a prelude to the wedding next day of Tom Cullen [the assistant director of intelligence] ... Dick Mulcahy ...was quiet in comparison with a number of the others and was not drinking and left early.

This was very different to the Cork atmosphere ... Brandy, champagne, whiskey in plenty and at 4:30 in the morning there were two sober men, Collins and I. I had to put most of them to bed.

When Leahy finally sat down with Collins, he was ordered to go to London and obtain a passport, which was issued in the name of a clerical student. He then made his way to Italy, travelling by way of Paris where he met the Sinn Féin emissary Seán T. O'Kelly who lived in a suite at the opulent *Le Grand Hotel*. It was even said that when he entered the dining room the hotel orchestra would strike up an Irish air.

Leahy reached Genoa in March and contacted Donal Hales, from Bandon, County Cork, who was in correspondence with Michael Collins, a friend of his brother's. Hales was the consul and trade representative for the 'Irish Republic' with an office in a sixteenth century *palazzo*. Affixed to the wall was a brass plaque inscribed with the words *Consolare*

Generale and *Agente Consolare Commerciale della Repubulica Irlandese.*

In addition to his job as a teacher, Hales wrote articles in leading newspapers, including Benito Mussolini's *Il Popolo d'Italia*, about 'British atrocities in Ireland'. Additionally he had ingratiated himself with a group of influential clerics and right wing politicians – ranging from Archbishop Ambrogio Ratti to Mussolini. In 1922, the former became Pope Pius XI and the latter Il Duce.

After the Great War he recognised that developments in Italy were to Ireland's advantage. The country had fought on the side of the Allies, but there was outrage over the Treaty of Versailles, with popular opinion convinced that Italy had received insufficient territorial rewards. Nationalists blamed their misfortune on British 'duplicity' and yearned to support the IRA against their new 'arch enemy'.

Hales decided that the stockpiles of weapons left over after the war were his for the asking. He approached Mussolini who brokered a meeting between him and officials from the War Department in Rome, where he was assured that they were prepared to supply the IRA. To conceal the transaction the weaponry would be classified as 'scrap' and sold for a 'nominal sum'. Additionally through his contacts in the Seafarers' Union, Donal was offered the use of a merchant vessel the *Stella Maris* (or Star of the Sea, a byname for Our Lady).

Hales wrote to Michael Collins urging him to purchase, what he called 'furniture' and 'antiques', and after Collins sent out two emissaries he gave the go ahead.

With the arrival of Mick Leahy, the pair put the finishing

touches to the operation. They inspected the *Stella Maris*; a four-masted sailing ship or barque, equipped with an auxiliary engine, and requiring a crew of ten. The vessel regularly imported coal from Newcastle; however on the outbound voyage from Genoa she travelled without a cargo except for a load of ballast to provide stability.

The plan was that the *Stella Maris* would embark from Genoa – without ballast and with Leahy on board as chief engineer and pilot – for the mouth of the Tiber near Rome, where the munitions would be secretly transferred from lighters. With the weapons substituting for ballast, the ship's waterline would provide no clue to any inquisitive British agent who happened to be on the shore. Then she would sail across the Mediterranean, through the Straits of Gibraltar and north towards Britain, before making a detour to the coast of Cork where the weaponry would be offloaded and then resume the voyage to Newcastle. In all a distance of around 4,000 kilometres.

The War Department confirmed that they would hand over 20,000 rifles, 500 machine guns and five million rounds of ammunition. The cost was £10,000, considerably less than the market value and well within the IRA's reach. Michael Collins passed word to Hales that 'the money would present no difficulty at all'. All he had to do was wait for a courier from Dublin; everything was ready to go.

In west Cork Liam Deasy took charge of the preparations. Working closely with the leadership of the Cork brigades, including Seán O'Hegarty and Tom Barry, he chose the vicinity of Myross Island as the most suitable location.

Myross was an isolated district far from any major police or army garrison and with a strong IRA presence. The area had an intricate network of minor roads and *boreens* (small unpaved country roads) providing multiple routes for the removal of the cargo. Additionally there was no single chokepoint that the British could hold and thereby prevent the IRA from escaping.

With Patrick O'Driscoll, the captain of the Myross Company as his guide, Deasy carefully surveyed the coastline by bicycle and boat and even made soundings as to the water's depth. By late April 1921 he had completed his plans.

As soon as the *Stella Maris* was sighted, a local fisherman would row out and join Leahy on board, he'd then pilot her through the narrow channel between Myross and Rabbit Islands, bringing her to anchor a few hundred metres from the shore. Behind Rabbit Island the ship would be hidden from the view of the Royal Navy sloop that regularly patrolled along the coast.

There were three adjacent sandy beaches suitable for landing the cargo. Without telling their owners what was afoot, Pat O'Driscoll arranged for a host of row boats, seventeen two-masted yawls and two motor-boats to be ready to sail out to the merchant ship. Having come alongside and clambering on board, the crews would lower hooks attached to ropes into the hold, raise the rifle and ammunition boxes onto the deck and then lower them over the side into the boats. At the beach the cargo would be hauled onto waiting horse-drawn carts together with any cars and lorries the IRA managed to seize and spirited off seventy kilometres to the north, to Seán O'Hegarty's headquarters in the Ballyvourney area. This was a massive heavy cargo and relays of relief horses were positioned along the route.

The roads leading to Myross were to be blocked by trenching, felling trees and demolishing bridges, with only the IRA convoy knowing the passable route. While O'Hegarty's and Barry's columns would cover the landing site. Elsewhere throughout Cork units were to make diversionary attacks, drawing the army and Auxiliaries away from the landing site.

As the cargo moved north, local battalions were to be mobilised to safeguard its passage. Scouts were to be posted at high points, equipped with horns or signal flags to warn of the approach of an enemy patrol. Finally at Ballyvourney the spoils were to be divided. The Cork brigades were to get their share, a portion was to be sent west to Kerry and the remainder onto Limerick and Tipperary and from there to the rest of the country. No wonder there was considerable excitement throughout Cork and in the words of one officer: 'By God but we'll bate them into the sea when we land that stuff.'

Deasy also made a backup plan in the event that British activity prevented him from removing the ordnance from Myross and he had scores of concealed arms dumps built locally. The dumps were equipped with boxes to protect the weapons from the dirt and damp and due to the scarcity of suitably treated wood even the floorboards of the Church of Ireland parish hall in Drimoleague were stolen. One of the largest dumps, capable of holding 200 rifles, was in an old ruined building with the hiding place concealed by moss-covered stones. Other dumps were made by digging into ditches and covering the openings with earth and sods.

The operation was coming together nicely.

In Italy Leahy and Hales waited for the £10,000 to arrive. In the meantime, they met with leading fascists, including several ex-army officers who were eager to return with him and fight the British.

George Gavan Duffy, a Sinn Féin diplomat in Europe, came through Genoa, and had Leahy reserve him a suite at the magnificent Bristol Palace Hotel. Leahy was flabbergasted with his insistence on (what he regarded as the epitome of luxury) a bathroom en suite. By then, he was disgusted with the extravagant lifestyle of some of the republican leadership.

Leahy became increasingly concerned: 'time passed and soon began to drag as I began to worry. The arms were available in plenty and were to be had, not for the asking, but for the money, and no money was coming from Ireland. In fact, no dispatch about any part of the plan was arriving … Madge, a sister of Donal Hales [and courier for Collins] came out to him on a holiday but she had no information for us either.' Eventually with his money running low he was forced to return home in April.

Back in Dublin 'I contacted the bold Mick and he claimed that they didn't send money out to me because I was being followed [by British agents].' Collins' contention was certainly credible. By then the plan to import arms was known to a few dozen people, including prominent members of Sinn Féin, senior IRA officers and multiple collaborators in Italy. Indeed Gen. Macready reported: 'information has been received from London and through the Admiral Commander-in-Chief, the Western Approaches [Ernest Gaunt] that 250,000 rifles have been purchased by Sinn Fein agents in Italy … and that these arms were loaded at Genoa … for Ireland. No sign of the ship or ships has been seen by the navy'. Macready commented that 'if the story is true I consider it important', adding that he awaited verification.

While this demonstrated that British intelligence were aware of the approaches made by Donal Hales and others to the Italian authorities, the information was incorrect in a number of facts and also omitted critical details such as: what ship or ships would transport the weaponry, when would they embark and where would they sail to in Ireland. Furthermore, although Collins might have found out that British agents were onto Hales and Leahy, he would not have seen Macready's report.

Leahy decided that the real reason why the operation was called off was 'that GHQ did not want arms. I was sent out only to keep the south quiet and especially Cork No. 1'. He elaborated: 'It is possible that he (Collins) was simply playing for time so that with the [Irish] people tired of war and the IRA unable to procure any arms and ammunition from Headquarters, the way would then be clear to settle with Britain for something much less than a republic.'

Leahy's reasoning was highly plausible. When Collins committed to the plan in 1920, he was determined to force the British to the negotiating table. Whereas by the time he withdrew his support a ceasefire was becoming increasingly likely and his priority was to encourage commanders such as O'Hegarty to settle for – what would inevitably be – a compromise peace.

In order to bolster his argument for a truce Collins claimed that by the summer of 1921 the IRA was effectively beaten and (somewhat ironically) was out of arms and ammunition; contending that 'the IRA could only have survived for another three weeks.' This may have been true of the Dublin brigades whose activities were badly mismanaged by GHQ, but the Cork fighters vehemently rejected the argument, with Tom Barry stating: '[the IRA] was a stronger and more effective force ... than at any other period in its history' adding with characteristic bluster that his flying column could have remained active for another five years. Seán Moylan commander of the North Cork Brigade was of a similar view.

Despite the collapse of the Italian operation, there was no let up in Collins' efforts to import munitions by other routes. Patrick Daly, an IRB operative at Liverpool docks, explained that 'there was no cessation of activity in connection with arms purchases during the Truce. I continued to be supplied with funds from Dublin and to receive orders from Collins ... My activity on that work did not cease until the beginning of 1922.' But these weapons were destined for Dublin where Collins would be able to maintain control of them and prevent them from falling into the hands of potential rivals.

It's strange that Collins never explained to the southern leadership why the operation was called off. Liam Deasy and

Tom Barry, who were both highly respected at GHQ, said that they received no explanation. The influential Florence O'Donoghue stated: 'I do not know why the project failed in Italy.' If Collins knew that the British had uncovered the plot then he should have shared this information with the Cork commanders, rather than largely remaining silent and thereby implicating himself. The evidence suggests that even though the British intelligence were aware of IRA efforts to procure arms in Italy they didn't possess specific actionable information.

There were two major consequences of the failure in Genoa. Firstly, it added to the already considerable distrust between Collins and the Cork IRA. In the words of Meda Ryan, 'seeds of discontent were sown at this period which were to spring to life later.' Secondly, it became obvious to O'Hegarty that if he wanted to acquire arms and ammunition, he had no one to depend upon but himself.

O'Hegarty was at his best when he was backed into a corner. He would put all the planning and preparation to good use: the arrangements to unload the ship, to protect the landing site, to evacuate and disperse the weapons, the construction of arms dumps, the hijacking of trucks and impressment of drivers.

The Italian Job proved to be a dry run.

7

QUEENSTOWN, 1921

Admiral Gaunt took command in Queenstown on the inauspicious date of 1 April 1921. There he held the title of Commander-in-Chief of the Western Approaches, which was a holdover from the Great War and nominally made him responsible for safeguarding 65,000 square kilometres of ocean to the west and south of Britain and Ireland. However, now that the war was over, his duties entailed overseeing the navy and the coastguard in Ireland, preventing arms smuggling and transporting the army's troops and equipment.

Gaunt worried that the coastguard stations were 'practically at the mercy of the rebels who can burn them down without interference' and the IRA had raided several looking for weapons and explosives. He complained that the customs service had collapsed in the face of intimidation: 'the present officials may be regarded as useless for the detection of arms. They are in too much bodily fear for themselves and their families to take action'. To prevent arms smuggling he and General Macready collaborated on a draconian proposal to blockade the entire island by closing the ports, which was never implemented.

He recommended to the government that warships should visit ports throughout Ireland to 'show the flag ... [and] give confidence to loyalists and waverers'. This slightly idiotic idea epitomised how out of touch he had become. On the other hand, he had more success running Haulbowline naval dockyards, where he was particularly proud of the apprenticeship programme, which provided locals with valuable skills.

As a port-based admiral he spent most of his time on administrative tasks, which he hated compared to being at sea and despite the seniority of his appointment he found himself sidelined. Macready boasted: 'the navy has for a very long time been working, I will not say under me, for that might hurt the senior service, but has been working in very close conjunction under my advice'.

The Gaunt's home was Admiralty House, a fine though unimposing three-storey building with a commanding view of Cork Harbour. And on a clear day Ernest enjoyed stepping out onto the two-storey cast iron veranda at the rear. Before him was a magnificent panorama of inlets, bays and islands interspersed with verdant promontories and headlands. Ships, large and small glided silently to and fro. There were merchant vessels and colliers sailing to England, a passenger ship on her way to Fishguard and boats transporting workers and supplies within the harbour.

In the distance was the harbour mouth; delineated on the east side by a short skinny peninsula with Roches Point lighthouse and coastguard station atop. To the west was a steep headland and in between was a narrow channel, two and a half kilometres long, which opened out into the harbour proper. The entrance was guarded by three forts: Templebreedy, Carlisle and Camden.

In front of Ernest and close to the shore there were three small islands: Spike, Haulbowline and Rocky Islands. Spike had a gentle grassy hill, on the top of which was Fort Westmoreland. During times of unrest it doubled as a prison and by 1921 it held 1,400 IRA prisoners.

A little west of Spike and half a kilometre offshore from Queenstown was Haulbowline, the major naval installation in Ireland. The partially reclaimed island was flat, low lying and almost completely paved over, with extensive wharfage lining the north and east shores. In the centre was a huge ships' basin and dry docks complex, built to accommodate battleships, which practically bisected the island. Towering over it was a massive crane, designed for hoisting and re-placing heavy naval guns. Close by there were six enormous store-houses, and behind these were large fuel tanks. On the western side of the island supplies and ordnance for the army were kept in warehouses, 'containing practically the whole of the reserve stores for the troops in Ireland'.

The island housed numerous workshops, including a metal foundry, an army and RIC barracks and at least two military hospitals, one of which specialised in tropical diseases for patients shipped back from the colonies. There was also the apprentices' school which Mick Leahy had attended.

Here warships underwent major repairs and refitting, others were resupplied and supply vessels arrived from England laden with war *matériel* for the army and RIC. This was where Gaunt had assumed command of *HMS Cambrian* in 1905 after it had been provisioned for three months at sea.

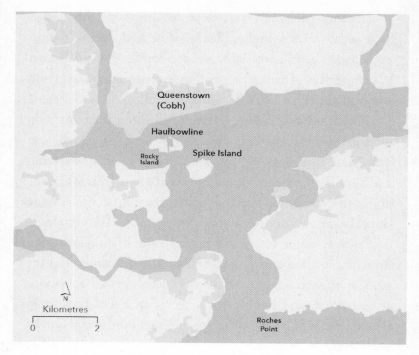

CORK'S LOWER HARBOUR

During the Great War the shipyards employed up to 3,000 personnel, many of whom were IRA members or sympathisers.

Haulbowline was a hive of intrigue. One of Gaunt's predecessors Admiral Lewis Bayly admitted: '[if] all persons of doubtful loyalty were to be discharged ... [it] would result in stopping all work in the dockyard.' Volunteers continually stole small quantities of weaponry, mainly from ships undergoing repair, or made gun and bomb parts in the workshops. And when Mick Murphy, of Cork No. 1, was employed as a carpenter he managed to walk off with three rifles.

On the southern edge of Haulbowline a causeway ran over to tiny Rocky Island, which in the nineteenth century had been hollowed out to construct two magazines capable of storing 25,000 barrels of gunpowder. In Gaunt's time it was used for 'the storage of small arms ammunition and ammunition for naval and military guns of various calibres, and is [sic] the only ordnance depot for gun ammunition in the south of Ireland.'

To the west of the islands was the narrow channel of the River Lee which led to the shallower upper harbour with Cork city and its docks.

Cork Harbour was so vast that it was said that during the days of sail up to 600 ships could shelter there. By the twentieth century, transatlantic liners anchored close to the entrance, while the naval moorings lay on the eastern side and between Haulbowline and Queenstown. During the war scores of British and American destroyers packed the area, but by 1921 there was only a single cruiser, together with a few destroyers and sloops.

Immediately in front of Admiralty House, its manicured gardens sloped down towards the water. And although Queenstown lay just beyond, it was nestled into the hillside and hidden from view, except for a row of protruding chimneys. In fact, the town's entire waterfront was invisible from the house including the Deepwater Quay.

It was only when Ernest crossed over to Haulbowline and looked back that he got a view of Queenstown, with its population of 8,200. Outwardly it resembled a picturesque nineteenth century English seaside town – it was even named in honour of Queen Victoria who landed there in 1849 – but in fact it was a major hub of IRA activity.

The colourfully painted houses were arranged in rows that followed the contours of the hill. In the centre of the town St Colman's cathedral with its tall spire dominated the scene. Here Louise and her children attended Catholic mass accompanied by a bodyguard of Royal Marines. A little to the east and on higher ground was Admiralty House, which appeared puny compared to the church.

Numerous quays, piers and landing spots lined the water-front. On the western edge of the town immediately adjacent to the train station was the Deepwater Quay. Close by was the town centre with Scott's Square and King's Square side by side. Behind the former was the RIC barracks on West View and on the corner of King's Square was the Rob Roy Hotel – a well-known IRA safe house – with its ornate and distinctive timber facade.

East of the town's squares were the thriving businesses lining West and East Beach with colourful canvas awnings overhanging the street which was open on one side to the ocean. On the waterside of East Beach there was an elegant single storey building with a tall clock tower, containing the offices of the King's Harbour Master, Capt. Usborne, who was in charge of the movements of all civilian vessels in the harbour. Further on was Lynch's Quay, with the red brick Custom House and a three-storey building which was the offices of Andrew Horne, Steamship Broker and Lloyd's Agents. Horne was a prominent businessman, desperate not to fall foul of either the British authorities or the IRA

QUEENSTOWN (COBH), 1921

Admiralty House

St Coleman's Cathedral

Harbour Row

Lynch's Quay

A. C. Horne
Shipbroker

Harbour
Master's
Office

East Beach

Harbour Hill

Cathedral Place

Rahilly Street

West Beach

King's Square

Rob Roy Hotel

Scott's Square

Westbourne Place

Spy Hill

Haulbowline Island
Royal Navy Yards

Railway
Station

Deep Water Quay

N

0   100
Metres

91

– a feat that was becoming increasingly more difficult.

At the far eastern end of town was the red light district, known as the Holy Ground, which was conveniently overlooked by the army barracks at Belmont Hutments.

The IRA had spies and informants throughout Queenstown, including a number in highly sensitive positions. There was Sgt John Maher at the RIC barracks on West View, who regularly warned the IRA of any impending raid, Jack Kilty and Philip O'Neill who were employed by the admiralty as clerks and a wounded British army veteran, by the name of O'Sullivan (with a brother in the IRA) who worked in the admiral's office at Admiralty House. There was also a mysterious figure at Haulbowline by the name of De Courcy who later proved to be of considerable value.

The most formidable IRA operative in Queenstown was its local commander Mick Burke – whom the *New York Times* once called the 'most terrible man in Ireland'. A grocer's assistant by trade, he led many successful attacks against the army and RIC. And even though he deliberately avoided targeting the navy's personnel, he proved to be a major headache for Admiral Gaunt.

In May 1921, Burke and eight volunteers snuck on board seven naval vessels, including five sloops, anchored in the harbour. They smashed the watertight doors with sledge-hammers and opened the sea cocks (the valves in the hull) thereby flooding the boats. The next morning when Burke stood on the shore he claimed: 'the only things visible were the masts and funnels of the vessels'

A few weeks later Burke discovered that the destroyer

HMS *Trenchant*, which was undergoing a refit at Haulbow-line, was afterwards scheduled to escort the sloop *Heather* as it transferred a group of IRA prisoners to Belfast Jail. To thwart the plan he enlisted two volunteers, Donal Collins and Jack Clarke, who worked at the shipyard and handed them five kilograms of gelignite along with detailed instructions. In the evening when it came time to finish work, they placed the explosives on board the *Trenchant* beside the engine and set a candle to light the fuse in about two hours. Sure enough at 7:30 p.m. a tremendous explosion rocked the dockyard and was heard across the town.

The next morning – much to the amusement of the IRA – Gaunt unwittingly choose one of the perpetrators, Donal Collins to help him inspect the ship. This revealed 'much damage' to the boiler and the steel armour plating of the hull, so the *Trenchant* had to be sent to Plymouth for repairs. Gaunt was so rattled that he closed the yard for almost two weeks. But Michael Burke was not yet finished with Gaunt and eventually the pair would come face to face.

Around the same time, Mick Murphy found out that Gaunt planned to travel to Cork by motorboat to meet with Gen. Strickland. Murphy set an ambush along the southern bank of the River Lee on the outskirts of the city. He positioned his riflemen and a Lewis machine gunner in concealed positions and they lay in wait ready to rake the boat and finish off the admiral. However, Gaunt had a stroke of luck when at the last moment he went by car instead.

Ernest and Louise lived in Queenstown with their two

daughters, twelve year old Sheila and six year old Yvonne. Their eldest John, who was sixteen, was a boarding student at the prestigious Oratory School in England and only visited during the holidays.

Sheila was Ernest's favourite. She was a bright and precocious girl with a mischievous sense of humour. Ernest and Sheila adored each other, in part because of that intense bond that fathers and daughters often have, but also out of a shared love for the Royal Navy. They were enthralled by its pageantry and pomp, its power and tradition. For them the navy was proof of British exceptionalism. Furthermore they both lived with chronic pain and had learned to support each other. He from his shattered left thigh bone, because of the fighting in Somalia, while she suffered from brittle bone disease (or osteogenesis imperfecta), resulting in her frequently breaking bones from the least trauma.

Louise regarded Sheila's illness as 'an embarrassing imperfection' and after the doctors – following the prevailing opinion of the time – blamed the mother for transmitting the disease, she shunned her daughter. A decision made all the easier since Sheila – by her own admission – had grown up to be rather plain looking. According to Sheila: 'Mother took this [my illness] to be a personal insult … after all she was a perfectionist. To have produced a flawed child was something she found impossible to accept … On the other hand the tie between father and myself became closer than ever. In fact he took over completely.'

Sheila looked forward to evenings when Ernest would made cocoa on the portable stove he kept in her bedroom and sitting at the end of the bed tell her about his adventures. There was the time when as a young lieutenant he set off in a row boat during a fierce storm off the Siberian coast in a valiant attempt to save his comrades whose boat had capsized. The *Times* praised his 'gallant efforts'. Or when he visited Tonga and King George Tupou II joined him for lunch on board *HMS Cambrian*. Sheila lay their enthralled: 'what bliss this was' she recalled.

In her 'house on the hill' Lady Gaunt lived a life under siege. Though secure in her fortified home, she was unable to move freely about the town. In the words of Sheila: 'I remember so well keeping vigil with mother when he [Ernest] was absent. The smell of fear from a very brave woman, never frightened for herself, but very much so for the husband she loved so dearly.' As always in times of trouble she sought refuge in her faith; fervently praying to the saints for their intercession and protection.

Despite her predicament Louise provided a warm welcome to visiting army and navy officers. She was a charismatic host and according to her daughter she had 'the most wonderful quality in making life exciting and fun'.

Aside from a token of appreciation she required little in return, though her patience was sorely tested by a navy captain who after an extended stay sent her half a salmon. As Sheila related: 'Admiralty House rang with the outraged cries of mother who was absolutely furious. If he had sent me a whole salmon, but half after six weeks of my lavish entertaining, she shrieked. Admiralty House rocked with these repercussions which everyone enjoyed.' On the other hand she was delighted when General Sir Nevil Macready stayed one night and presented her with a 'most enormous gorgonzola cheese'. Though the general remarked cryptically: 'My cheese resembles a battlefield with the Shinners under fire and hopping in all directions'.

Louise and Ernest regaled their guests with tales of their travels and exploits. Louise often repeated her story about the time when, accompanying Ernest, she became the first white woman to visit a Pacific island reputedly inhabited by 'cannibals'. Or when the Ottoman Sultan awarded her the Order of Shefkat – 'a truly magnificent bauble of precious stones' – for lecturing the ladies of the harem on the subject of child rearing.

Ernest was a seasoned raconteur with a dry sense of humour, whose anecdotes had a moral underpinning, often something to do with duty and honour. He had a lot of wisdom to share and he was determined to do so. In his own words, he was 'a salt water soaked admiral, soaked from stem to stern … [With a career spent] visiting every land, in ruling and conferring with rulers, in serving and studying service, in combating the forces of nature and machinations of man'. Occasionally he would point out the chunk of steel hanging on the wall of the dining room, which was a fragment of *HMS Colossus* and launch into an account of the Battle of Jutland.

Admiral Gaunt and his guests were unanimous that the IRA was cowardly and ill-disciplined; 'a horde of rebels' and blackguards responsible for all sorts of savagery. They were critical of what they regarded as the government's timid response, notwithstanding its deployment of the Black and Tans and Auxiliaries. But they were forced to adopt that attitude, because if the government was not to blame for the inability to defeat the IRA, then it had to be their fault. Ernest himself complained – 'thanks politicians, for having us fight the enemy with one hand behind our backs' – and he claimed he knew of an intelligence officer who 'was caught and castrated by the IRA'.

Gen. Sir Peter Strickland was a frequent visitor, often driving over from Cork city for lunch followed by a game of mixed doubles tennis. A strict disciplinarian, his men knew him as 'old hungry face'. Despite Seán O'Hegarty having made several attempts to kidnap and kill him, Strickland knew little about the elusive O'Hegarty other than he was 'the murderer' of his friend Mrs Lindsay and a leader of the 'rabble' or 'mock army'.

Gen. Macready declared: 'I loathe the country … and its people with a depth deeper than the sea and more violent than that which I feel against the Boche [Germans]'. Adding that 'a people characterized through past centuries by lack of discipline, intolerance of restraint and with no common standard of public morality'… [could] only be governed and held in check under the protection of a strong military garrison'. He believed that IRA volunteers were paid for 'each murder carried through'.

One naval officer thought that gangsters from Chicago were reinforcing the IRA. Maj. Bernard Law Montgomery, who often visited Ernest and Louise, argued 'it never bothered me a bit how many houses were burnt [in reprisals].

I think I regarded all civilians as Shinners … to win a war of this sort you must be ruthless … the Germans would have settled it in a very short time.'

Their mindset was formed by years of colonial service and was well summed up by one officer who wrote: 'Sinn Féin [the IRA] is made up of the scum of Ireland, who could not be expected to fight fair or square like men'. This attitude led Gaunt to underestimate the challenges he faced in Ireland.

In June 1921, Louise and Ernest enjoyed a respite when they travelled by warship to Belfast to welcome King George V and Queen Mary. The royal yacht *Victoria and Albert* sailed into Belfast Lough accompanied by a squadron of battleships and their majesties came ashore at Donegall Quay, to be greeted by a twenty-one-gun salute, the din of dozens of ships' sirens and wild cheering. The king, dressed as an Admiral of the Fleet, was met by a host of dignitaries including Admiral Gaunt and Gen. Macready and a guard of honour of Royal Marines, resplendent in their scarlet uniforms. The royal couple then travelled by open carriage to city hall – Gaunt riding behind in a chauffeur driven car – with an escort of mounted cavalry from the 10th Hussars; the route was lined by a throng of tens of thousands and was bedecked with union jack flags and bunting.

In the evening the king gave a speech calling for peace and reconciliation between loyalists and nationalists: 'I pray with earnest confidence and hope that in the era which now opens there will be readiness on all sides to work in harmony for the common good.'

Later on Ernest and Louise joined their majesties on

board their yacht for lunch. Ernest and George V got on tremendously well; aside from their fervent belief in the empire and their disdain for high culture and intellectual pursuits, they both revered the navy. The king enjoyed reminding his admiral of the time they spent 'in the same term' at cadet school on *HMS Britannia*, although Ernest was reluctant to point out that his majesty was actually in the year ahead.

Gaunt was enormously proud that during the Battle of Jutland, the king's favourite son Prince Albert (later George VI) served under his command as a sub-lieutenant. He took it as a vote of confidence in his wise and astute leadership that his majesty had entrusted the safety of his sickly (and constantly sea sick) prince to his care.

They discussed the quagmire in Ireland and their future hopes for the navy. While to Louise's delight the queen, in a moment of casual intimacy, said: 'I hope Lady Gaunt you never forget your gloves, they are such a help when shaking all those sweaty palms.' Sitting there and chatting with the queen, Gerry Martyn had come a long way from her childhood in County Clare.

As the Gaunt's returned to Cork by ship the 10th Hussars, who had accompanied the king's procession in Belfast, departed for Dublin by train. Unfortunately the IRA laid a mine on the tracks, derailing the train and killing four Hussars and two railway employees, while eighty horses were either killed or had to be put down.

On 7 July, the Gaunts attended a state ball at Buckingham Palace. Four days later Sinn Féin and the British agreed to a truce. Finally, Ernest and Louise could anticipate an end to their assignment in Cork.

8

THE CORK REPUBLIC

Although rumours had been swirling for months, the announcement of the Anglo-Irish Truce came as a great surprise. Florence O'Donoghue reported: 'The whole country is gone mad, cheering, shouting and so forth'. In Cork city 'the citizens played holiday round their streets until well past midnight each night, rejoicing in their new found liberty'. Even 'the RIC and the Tans strolled around aimlessly and at ease'.

Finally, the IRA appeared out in the open. Frank O'Connor of Cork No. 1 wrote: 'all that perfect summer young men who had been for years in hiding drove around the country in commandeered cars, drinking, dancing, brandishing their guns'. A brigade officer, Michael O'Donoghue, remembered: "Twas hard, even for the IRA themselves to credit that the fortunes of war had changed to such an extent. We could now move everywhere in town and country. We exulted in our new found authority and importance.'

Christopher O'Keeffe was struck by the dramatic change in attitude of the Black and Tans: 'After the Truce many of those who beat us up, or witnessed the beatings, came along and requested our photographs for, as they remarked, "the gallant stand we made".'

Seán O'Hegarty hurriedly returned to the city from Ballyvourney. He welcomed the ceasefire, but he only wanted a short one. Without a Republic, he remained a man on a mission and it was time to reorganise, rearm, recruit and train in preparation for the final push. According to Mick Murphy: 'Seán O'Hegarty was most determined and he was always lecturing us about the fight being renewed'.

After a few days of 'rejoicing and relaxation' the IRA were back at work. William Crowley of Skibbereen remembered: 'when the Truce was signed there was a general relaxation of tension for a few days. However, inside a week, the work of organisation was taken up again.'

O'Hegarty ran training camps throughout his area and held special courses on machine gun handling, explosives, engineering and signalling. He led an all-out effort to stockpile explosives, hand grenades and landmines, in the process overseeing five clandestine metal foundries. Fitters, blacksmiths and other skilled workers volunteered their services and machinery and heavy tools were commandeered from the Port of Cork, the Cork Power Company and the Ford Tractor Factory. Tons (thousands of kilograms) of homemade explosives were hidden away in secure dumps.

As always Seán was thorough. Roads were trenched and obstructed, while potential ambush positions were scouted out and readied. Daniel Corkery from Macroom reported: 'orders were issued to mine roads at suitable ambush positions and to prepare bridges on all roads for demolition by explosive charges. These precautions were taken to ensure that our columns could take the initiative at short notice.'

However, Seán had little success in procuring arms and ammunition. It was no longer feasible to use the army and police as a source and aside from six or so Thompson submachine guns smuggled in from America there was only the steady trickle of small caches into Cork.

Outwardly Michael Collins agreed with O'Hegarty that the Truce provided a temporary respite. In a conversation with Collins, a senior IRA officer James Malone came away with the impression 'that the Truce was just a ploy to give the IRA a chance to have a rest ... Just as soon as we were ready, with sufficient guns and ammunition, the war would be resumed all over again.' Collins told Seán MacBride, a young staff officer: 'We can use it to reorganise and to get more arms in' and in a classic example of his double speak added 'I want you to start working on that immediately.' Seán Moylan concurred: 'Word was passed around from Headquarters in Dublin that the Truce might break any moment'.

But O'Hegarty was well attuned to Collins' smooth talk and at a meeting held in Cork 'Michael Collins talked at a great rate ... Seán O'Hegarty put up his finger and said, "Don't talk so fast for we can't write so fast and we want to write it all down".' With that Collins went quiet. But despite Collins' evasiveness O'Hegarty came away convinced that he was prepared to accept a settlement that fell short of a sovereign republic.

Meanwhile Collins and Risteárd Mulcahy attempted to marginalise the hard-nosed O'Hegarty and replace him with someone more compliant. Mulcahy proposed to Mick Leahy that Cork No. 1 should be split into two, with Leahy taking charge of the city and Queenstown and what remained left under Seán's command. However when the brigade officers met everyone, including Leahy, stood behind Seán forcing GHQ for once to back down.

The British observed the IRA's increasingly open activity with mounting concern, seeing their enemy appear to go from strength to strength. Strickland reported: 'Rebel military organisation have [sic] everywhere been consolidated ... arms have been landed in large quantities.'

But, the opposite was actually happening and by the autumn discipline within the IRA was collapsing. In the words of Dan Gleeson, from Tipperary: '[The Truce] was a pause, but not a victory. Unfortunately the great bulk of the lads thought they had won.' Seán Moylan warned that it 'was now a period of relaxation, when the discipline which physical danger imposes had disappeared and when men had to face the more subtle danger of fleeting flattery and adulation.'

Michael O'Donoghue of Cork No. 1 admitted: 'We were youngsters in our teens and early twenties and who could blame us if we got intoxicated with all the hero worship and rejoicings.' Once after a dance, he fired his revolver into the air to impress his female companions. Another time he crashed his car into a horse drawn cab on St Patrick's Bridge in the city and when the jarvey demanded compensation, O'Donoghue 'showed him the butt of my automatic and told him to clear. He shut up instantly and mounting his cab drove off'.

Incidences of anti-social behaviour and outright criminality dramatically increased; 'drinking, freeloading and commandeering of cars became commonplace'. Houses and shops were robbed, civilians were threatened and occasionally shot. GHQ complained 'drinking among our men has come to the point of scandal'.

In Tipperary, an off-duty RIC officer was shot in the head. In Midleton Mick Leahy discovered that the volunteers were stealing from brigade funds and from locals to pay for drink. 'They had terrorised the people' reported Leahy. Even Macready's jaundiced view was correct when he said: 'the rank and file of the IRA are losing popularity ... owing to the fact that numbers of them have done no work since July 11th, but are billeted in good houses and practically live on the country.'

And though Seán O'Hegarty and his 'crowd' remained as steadfast and determined as ever, it became increasingly difficult to hold his brigade together with many volunteers drifting away.

Eventually in October a Sinn Féin delegation, which included Michael Collins, went to London for the final round of negotiations. Collins brought with him his reputation for heavy drinking and carousing and he soon came under the spell of the beautiful Hazel Lavery – a socialite and wife of the painter John Lavery – with whom it was widely believed he was having an affair. O'Hegarty got word of 'alleged orgies' and he complained to Mulcahy of Collins: being the ringleader at drunken parties where furniture and doors were smashed, of running up a weekly drinks' bill of hundreds of pounds and being frequently hung over. Though O'Hegarty was unable to substantiate his claims when Mulcahy demanded evidence.

The Irish delegates – regarded by the British government

as 'children in statesmanship and politics' – signed the Anglo-Irish Treaty on 6 December under the threat of renewed 'terrible and immediate war'. The treaty granted the Irish Free State significant independence, similar to that of the dominions of Canada and Australia, with full fiscal control and its own army. However, it was less than a sovereign republic and the king remained head of state. Bowing to reality, Ireland was to be partitioned with most of Ulster remaining part of the United Kingdom.

Although the Treaty was enthusiastically received throughout Ireland, the majority of the IRA – who had been led to expect a complete separation from Britain – were stunned. Nowhere was the gulf between the attitude of the public and the IRA more glaring than in Cork. James Murphy, commander of the Macroom battalion, complained that 'the Republic which we had been fighting for had been abandoned and the country partitioned', while Daniel Corkery said that the IRA's reaction was one of 'profound disappointment'.

Some Cork republicans went so far as to accuse Collins of being a traitor. Mary MacSwiney, a Sinn Féin activist close to O'Hegarty, accused Collins of doing England's bidding: 'what service [he] rendered Ireland in earlier years was nullified by [his] later action.' Her sister-in-law Muriel said that the Treaty 'was the greatest, even personal tragedy that had befallen me up to that time', despite the fact that her husband Terence – who had been Lord Mayor of Cork – had died on hunger strike in a British prison only a year earlier.

Seán O'Hegarty was determined to scuttle the Treaty and he adopted 'the most belligerent course of action, breaking up public meetings, harassing local newspapers and suppressing pro-Treaty publications'. In his own words, he was opposing 'open enemies of the Republic and useless non-committals'. Liam de Róiste, who was a Sinn Féin Dáil deputy for the city and a supporter of the Treaty, complained: 'many of the fine clean honest, intelligent fellows who had been [IRA] officers from 1914 on, either resigned or were virtually dismissed'.

O'Hegarty was incensed when the London *Times* correspondent Arthur Kay visited Cork and interviewed a number of his officers including Capt. Éamon O'Mahony – the southern liaison officer with the British forces during the Truce period – whom he quoted as rhetorically asking: 'If we had to go to war again, what better terms should we win?'

Kay fled back to Dublin when he was threatened with imprisonment in Knockraha or as it was vividly described to him – that he'd be 'put in a vault with corpses and a candle'. Shortly afterwards he and two other journalists were having lunch in a pub, when all of a sudden Sandow O'Donovan and Mick Murphy burst in with automatics drawn. With Jim Gray – O'Hegarty's driver – waiting outside in a stolen Rolls Royce.

'Don't move or we'll blow your bloody brains out. Which one of you is Kay?' demanded Sandow. 'That's my name'. 'There's a car outside and if you don't get into it, by Christ, you'll be dead meat'. Sandow allowed Kay to finish his drink and they then briskly walked to the Rolls Royce. Across the street were four police officers on duty who took no notice. Sandow and Kay got in, while Murphy remained in Dublin.

Somewhat surprisingly the owner was still seated in the back and having driven a short distance Gray politely said to him 'I'll drop you off now'.

Jim Gray drove in a 'breakneck dash' with a terrified Kay in the back of 'that tossing, pitching, skidding car as it bumped and bounced its way towards Cork'. According to Kay: 'I have heard stories of derring-do in the matter of motor driving but I never met his equal.' At one stage when the car reached a particularly dangerous stretch of road, Gray turned around to him with 'an amicable grin on his face'.

Sandow and Gray joked that they were so 'fed up' searching all over for him that they felt like shooting him. But his captors turned out to be surprisingly good company and Kay said of Sandow: 'He did not boast, but he spoke with a matter of fact directness of deeds done which convinced me that he would carry out his orders and that if I attempted to escape not the slightest predilection in favour of a prisoner, apart from his sense of duty, would influence him. Though he was kindly and affable I never lost sight of the sinister looking gun which peeped out of his pocket. He was considerate asking if I was warm'. And with that, Sandow solicitously passed him a blanket.

Later they pulled into a pub to get a quick drink. They continued their journey, at times passing with impunity army and police lorries. After midnight they arrived at a remote farmhouse, where along with the farmer and his wife they all gathered around the peat fire for supper and a lively chat.

The following day Kay went for a ramble across the countryside with a local IRA officer, whom he declared was 'one of the most charming men in the world'. It wasn't until the afternoon that O'Hegarty and his entourage arrived in two cars. There seemed to be no sense of urgency and everyone sat down for tea in the kitchen, until eventually moving to the sitting room, which had been rearranged into an improvised courtroom. With Seán as prosecution and judge, Kay was charged 'with publishing news concerning the Irish Republican Army which had not been authorised and with the fact that the views put forth did not represent the views of the Army in Cork'.

O'Hegarty passed the defendant a copy of his article with the relevant passages marked in ink and proceeded to call on Éamon O'Mahony, who admitted he had a conversation with Kay, but denied it was a formal interview adding that the journalist hadn't taken notes. A second witness was 'unable to recall any of the statements made'.

With no evidence presented in his defence Kay was then sent into the kitchen while the court deliberated; waiting there it crossed his mind that they could pass the death sentence. After 'a very considerable interval', he was called back for the verdict. O'Hegarty pronounced that as O'Mahony was a liaison officer he was no longer an active IRA officer and therefore in the article he should not have been referred to as 'an officer of the IRA'. Kay was then offered the choice of issuing a statement clarifying these 'facts' or being deported. He chose the former.

A much relieved Kay was driven to Cork city and handed over to Collins' emissary Emmet Dalton, who had rushed down from Dublin. Kay was amused that unlike Jim Gray,

Dalton and his companions had great difficulty navigating the war ravaged roads. 'We entered Cashel and motored on for several miles only to find ourselves in the town again, and again [*sic*] we missed our way. Broken bridges, wrong turnings and many other accidents hindered us (the chauffeur on one occasion falling into a pool when in quest of water).' Finally, after a marathon sixteen hours he arrived back to the safety of the capital city.

The kidnapping was a major embarrassment for Collins, particularly since GHQ had guaranteed Kay's safety. In the middle of the crisis, O'Hegarty rubbed salt into the wounds by phoning Sinn Féin in Dublin to say that following a 'court of inquiry' Kay would be promptly released. While Michael Collins in an interview with the *Times* made the empty threat that the kidnappers would 'be severely punished'.

It's extraordinary that O'Hegarty orchestrated such an elaborate operation over what was to him a matter of honour and principle. This episode did little to endear him to Collins and Mulcahy whose powerlessness in the south he had clearly exposed.

Around the same time Seán issued a death threat to the Dáil deputies from Cork: 'you are reminded it is your duty to support this demand [to reject the Treaty]. To act otherwise would be treason to the Republic to which we have sworn allegiance'. And when a local *cumann* (branch) of Sinn Féin met to appoint delegates for a special meeting in Dublin, Sandow turned up declaring 'that if pro-Treaty candidates were selected they would not leave Cork alive'. Wisely the members chose Sandow as one of their delegates.

Risteárd Mulcahy called O'Hegarty's threat 'a most irregular interference' in political matters and demanded an apology. But O'Hegarty argued that 'the circumstances cannot be judged as the ordinary political variations of a settled country. Here is no ordinary political change. What is contemplated in these proposals is more than that, it is the upsetting of the constitution – the betrayal of the Republic.'

Finally on 7 January following weeks of – frequently vitriolic – debate the Dáil narrowly ratified the Treaty. Thereafter events unfolded rapidly. De Valera, who opposed the agreement, resigned as head of the government. An interim Provisional Government was set up with Collins as chairman and Minister of Finance and Mulcahy remained chief of staff of the IRA. Collins was now in control of both the political and military wings of the new state, at least until the formal establishment of the Irish Free State following a general election that would take place in the summer.

Although approximately 80% of the IRA rejected the settlement, Collins' clarity of vision and strategic sensibility allowed him to outmanoeuvre his divided and indecisive opponents and using Dublin as his stronghold he consolidated his position. The pro-Treaty IRA acquired the trappings (and eventually the weaponry) of a regular army and became known as the National Army.

The British turned over the reins of government to the Provisional Government, while the RIC were steadily disbanded and the army evacuated. At the same time, Macready resolved to prevent his forces being caught up in, what he called, the 'maelstrom of the opposing savages'.

These developments meant that by February 1922 Cork was largely cut off from the rest of the country and nowhere was this more apparent than in the city, where the Provisional Government exercised no authority and had no armed presence. The RIC were dispirited and largely disbanded and the army had withdrawn to barracks. Seán O'Hegarty and Cork No. 1 went unchallenged.

It was no wonder that people began to talk about the 'Cork Republic' and although the term was sometimes used whimsically, it was grounded in a certain reality. As early as the autumn of 1921 a journalist from the *New York Times* 'finds Sinn Féiners running Cork city … [they] are administering justice and carrying on all the affairs of the city'.

In February 1922, Gen. Macready wrote to Winston Churchill – who as Secretary of State for the Colonies had significant responsibility for Irish affairs – that 'the Republic exists in Cork and the surrounding country and that there is no sign or shadow of Provisional Government authority'. Adding: 'I think it quite possible that Collins and Co. will have to fight for their lives, not only with ballot boxes, but also with automatics and rifles.'

Peter Hart wrote: 'Only in Cork were there republican censors, tax collectors and even postage stamps all administered by the IRA, which constituted the sole real authority in the county', though adding with scepticism 'Of all the revolutionary regimes which emerged in Europe in the wake of the Great War, the Irish republic in Cork in 1922 was perhaps the least substantial and most curious. Republicans who opposed the treaty with England claimed that the whole island was an indivisible sovereign state, but in practice it was only in Cork and adjoining areas that they held effective power'.

Liam de Róiste – who regarded O'Hegarty and his crowd 'as a band of desperadoes running amok' – complained that 'there is neither law nor order now'. This deteriorating situation was highlighted by an incident that occurred in mid-February. At five o'clock one evening Lieut Henry Genochio left his quarters at Victoria Barracks and headed into town. He was dressed in civilian clothes and carried his revolver and identity badge in his pockets. What happened afterwards is unclear, but according to the IRA they arrested him that night for robbery and found him to be in possession of £15, a lady's handbag and several gold watches and chains. With the result that he was imprisoned in the city's (Eglington) Lunatic Asylum, which O'Hegarty had partially converted into a prison. Two days later, Genochio was seen running from the grounds of the asylum pursued by two guards, who shot him in the back. The RIC later recovered his body from the Lee Road.

All hell broke loose. Churchill was appalled: 'since when have the IRA the right to arrest British officers and shoot them if they try to escape? This callous and brutal murder cannot be left unpunished'. Genochio's father wrote to Churchill about the family's 'terrible grief' and 'not in any spirit of vindictiveness nor with any desire for revenge' sought justice.

Macready gave orders to raid the asylum and bring

the perpetrators to justice, until Strickland cautioned that he risked starting 'the war afresh'. To compound matters Macready found out that Genochio had been in financial difficulties and was about to be disciplined for not paying his mess bill. Forcing him to admit to his friend Field Marshal Sir Henry Wilson: 'I have heard some rather funny things about the case ... it looks very much as if for the sake of the boy and his people the less said about it the better' adding 'don't let MPs press the case'.

Michael Collins sent a telegram to Churchill saying that he was 'doing everything to discover the facts' of the case, which Macready regarded as all 'bosh, because Collins has no authority whatever down there at present.'

Churchill, Macready and Collins were all forced to accept that Cork was Seán O'Hegarty's fiefdom and whether they liked it or not, there was nothing they could do about it. At least not for now. It was no wonder that Henry Wilson wrote to Macready: 'The whole of that Irish situation leads to vomit!'

In the escalating stand off between the anti-Treaty IRA and Collins' Provisional Government, it was inevitable that unless either side was prepared to back down then there would be civil war. Seán O'Hegarty and his fighters were not prepared to accept the compromise of the Treaty. In their minds, it would be a betrayal of their oath to the Republic, to the memory of their dead and to that of the past generations of Irish patriots.

O'Hegarty knew that once the anti-Treaty IRA

committed itself to war then they had to wage it all out, giving no quarter. He 'was all out for ruthless warfare' and told his comrades: 'Either be prepared to cut all their throats, or leave them alone and go home'.

9

DE COURCY

Queenstown, with its vital docks and naval facilities, was one of the few southern towns where the British continued to maintain a strong military presence. Admiral Gaunt and Gen. Strickland oversaw the repatriation of the troops along with their equipment and soon the quays at Queenstown and nearby Cork were a hive of activity with soldiers embarking on ships and cargo being hoisted into waiting holds. Gen. Macready was determined to 'clear out every soldier and policeman as quickly as it possibly can be done and leave these people to settle their own affairs'.

One of Gaunt's primary responsibilities was conveying the vast quantity of munitions at Haulbowline and Rocky Islands to the Royal Navy's magazines at Devonport in Plymouth. There were rifles, revolvers, machine guns, mortars and artillery pieces, shells, explosives and up to a million of rounds of ammunition. Macready knowing that 'the town and county of Cork are at present in a very inflammable condition' resolved to keep this stuff from falling into the wrong hands.

Ernest brought over the Royal Fleet Auxiliary vessel *Upnor*, which was specifically designed to transport explosives and ammunition. She was built on the Clyde in 1899 and was forty-three metres in length with a black steel hull. Being a working ship, she wasn't spick and span like a warship and her rust stained paintwork could have done with a touch up, but despite this, with her long low profile she had certain elegance and almost looked graceful. Her most distinctive and important feature was a huge hold, comprising a single compartment, which ran from the bow to the midships. This resulted in the bridge, engine room and crews' quarters being pushed to the aft of the ship. Forward there was a steam-powered derrick for hoisting cargo in and out of the hold.

A three-pounder gun had been mounted at the bow during the war; its forty-seven millimetre calibre shells were more than enough to repulse any conceivable attack. There were also two rifles and one or two revolvers on board. For communications, the ship was dependent on flags or Morse signalling lamps, since she had no radio.

The *Upnor* had a crew of fourteen, under the command of Capt. J. Hoar, including a first mate, a technician trained in the handling and storage of high explosives, together with two engineers, three stokers and seven deck hands.

By February 1922, the ship was moored alongside the Haulbowline quays as her cargo was being loaded; it was a slow laborious process. Thousands of cases of small arms ammunition, shells and explosives together with crates of rifles, machine guns and revolvers were lowered into the hold and secured. Gaunt had instructed that the boxes of rifles and revolvers should be hidden under the other stores, but in the interest of expediency the supervising officer ignored him.

There were also 1,200 swords and sword bayonets and

even a collection of obsolete cannon balls. Finally, furniture and household goods belonging to officers and employees returning to England was piled up on the deck and also packed into a barge for the *Upnor* to tow. Everything needed to be precisely documented and written down in the ship's manifest.

The task required a great deal of care and expertise; if the explosives were manhandled, dropped or stored incorrectly it could set off an explosion and blow the ship and a considerable part of the dockyard to kingdom come. It must have been on everybody's mind that four years earlier the French munitions ship *Mont-Blanc* had been involved in a low speed, one knot (less than two kilometres per hour) collision in Halifax Harbour, Nova Scotia, resulting in a tremendous explosion that destroyed nearly every structure within a radius of 800 metres, killed 2,000, wounded 9,000 and even generated its own tsunami wave.

An inexperienced observer might have thought that these munitions were vulnerable to an IRA attack, but Ernest Gaunt knew that this was well-nigh impossible. It wasn't just that O'Hegarty's brigade didn't have the strength to seize the ship while it lay under heavy guard in the harbour, but they had no ability to capture her once she set sail. As he pointed out: 'the very large quantities of munitions in Ireland at the time the treaty was signed were brought to this country during the whole period of active operations without escort on the high seas having been considered necessary.'

Previously during the 'troubles' he had warned ship

captains to be vigilant and one of them even installed 'steel flexible hose pipes [which,] led to the upper deck direct from the boilers to pour scalding steam on any attackers'. But these precautions were for vessels at anchor in a remote bay or in an undefended harbour, whereas the *Upnor* was sailing from one protected naval base to another.

True, in the distant past – and often with the tacit approval of the English crown – piracy had been endemic along the Irish coast particularly in Cork. In 1617, Sir Henry Mainwaring, himself a former pirate, wrote that Ireland 'may be well called the nursery and storehouse of pirates'. But there hadn't been any incidents for over 200 years; one of the last attacks occurring when a French privateer, piloted by Irish exiles, sailed into Cork Harbour and in full view of the citizenry of (what was then known as) Cove, captured the customs officers and carried them off to 'l'arn them to spake French' as the locals said.

However, by 1922 the harbour was safe and secure. On Haulbowline the RIC and army: guarded the gates, patrolled the docks and searched workmen entering and leaving. Additionally there were 350 soldiers from the North Staffordshire Regiment at nearby Belmont Hutments and a detachment of twenty-nine Royal Marines protected Admiralty House.

But the security of the harbour ultimately depended on an integrated system of fortresses and observation posts, manned by a 500 strong force under the command of Maj. W. Parker of the Royal Garrison Artillery. From his headquarters at Queenstown Parker could direct a coordinated response within minutes against any intruder.

On the western promontory guarding the harbour entrance was Fort Templebreedy, which functioned as both a look out and an artillery battery. During the day it afforded a view far out to sea and at night it's searchlights swept the ocean below. It was equipped with two 9.2 inch (234 mm) calibre guns, capable of firing an explosive shell – weighing 170 kilograms – a range of over twenty-six kilometres. These powerful guns were designed to sink warships, including destroyers and cruisers. On the opposite side of the harbour mouth, Roches Point lighthouse and coastguard station had a look out and a wireless transmitter, but no artillery.

Just inside the narrow entrance channel was Fort Carlisle on the east and opposite lay Fort Camden. Carlisle was the more formidable and was equipped with two 9.2 inch and four 6 inch (152 mm) guns along with three 12 pounder (76 mm calibre) quick firing guns, capable of firing fifteen rounds a minute at a range of over ten kilometres. Camden was armed with five 12 pounder guns and a mounted machine gun.

Meanwhile Fort Westmoreland on Spike Island had an encasement of two 6 inch guns – with a range of up to fourteen kilometres – along with 12 pounder guns, covering the main expanse of the harbour.

The guns at Forts Carlisle, Camden and Westmoreland were supported by electrical lights and were capable of night fighting. Additionally all positions were reinforced by infantry detachments. Admiral Gaunt and Maj. Parker had ordered that 'guns are always to be kept ready for immediate

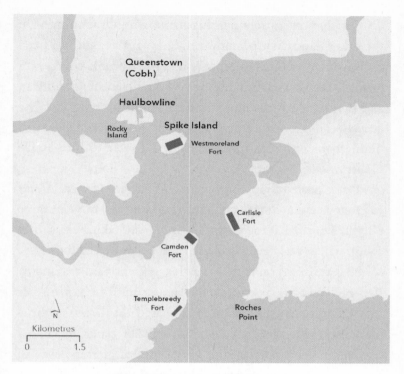

CORK HARBOUR DEFENCES

'action' and that 'a gun should be kept trained on an incoming vessel until she has been passed as friendly'.

But despite the strength of the harbour's defences the *Upnor*'s cargo must have aroused considerable interest among a workforce widely sympathetic to the IRA. One of those workers was a volunteer attached to C Company of the city's 1st Battalion, who was reputedly in charge of the stores on Haulbowline.

There's uncertainty as to who the informant was. According to Sandow O'Donovan – who had previously been

OC of the 1st Battalion – his name was 'de Courcy'. On the other hand, Mick Leahy said he was Alec Sullivan from Queenstown. While Sandow is a highly reliable source, it's possible that the agent was indeed Sullivan or O'Sullivan and that Sandow was protecting his identity, especially if he later became a recipient of a British government pension. Though for purposes of expediency I'll refer to him as De Courcy.

De Courcy first approached a brigade officer Peter O'Donovan who in turn contacted Sandow and he went on to tell them both 'that there was a possibility of taking arms from a ship which was being loaded at the wharf in Haulbowline'. Word was passed on to Seán O'Hegarty who said to Sandow that he 'would not consider the matter until he got further information.' After De Courcy procured the *Upnor*'s official manifest, O'Hegarty finally summoned a brigade council.

The meeting was held at his new headquarters, the All for Ireland Club, 6 Emmet Place in the heart of the city, situated between the north channel of the River Lee and St Patrick's Street and opposite the Opera House. In one of those typical O'Hegarty 'mysteries' the building had somehow been loaned, 'borrowed' or commandeered from the All for Ireland League which was a nationalist party associated with the Home Rule movement that had gone into terminal decline following the 1916 Rising and the subsequent ascent of Sinn Féin.

The Club fronted both Emmet Place and Drawbridge Street and had a side door that opened onto a small courtyard shared by multiple adjacent buildings. With its many escape routes this was the ideal lair for Seán who never wanted to be cornered 'in a bloody rat trap' during a raid.

Those who attended were members of his 'crowd', people he had long ago vetted, whom he trusted and who had earned the right to be trusted. All of them had spent years carrying out his orders – killing, raiding and ambushing – and nearly all had been imprisoned at one time or another. As Michael Collins said: 'once you passed the test by Seán O'Hegarty you were fit for anything'.

There was unanimous support for the idea of capturing the munitions, but the group had considerable difficulty coming up with a feasible plan. They might have had a slim chance of capturing the *Upnor*, but it was clearly impossible to unload her at Haulbowline. This was a job that would take a large workforce several hours to complete, during which time they would be vulnerable to attack.

The first plausible proposal was to raid Haulbowline, seize the *Upnor* and sail her up river to Cork, where she could be unloaded alongside the quays. This idea had a number of advantages: the brigade was well versed in the art of surprise attacks and in a short determined assault might be able to commandeer the vessel, the Cork dockers could be expected to help out and all the equipment needed to unload the ship was already in place on the city quays. It also availed of the fact that the British artillery defences were aimed in the direction of the harbour mouth and not towards the inner harbour.

But there were numerous flaws. Given the IRA's lack of arms and ammunition could they realistically overpower the guard on Haulbowline? If they somehow managed to take possession of the *Upnor* how could they sail her? Furthermore, the provocation of nabbing the *Upnor* and sailing her into Cork would be too great for Strickland to ignore, and he was sure to order a counter-attack from nearby Victoria Barracks, which would easily overwhelm the IRA.

The arguments raged back and forth. All the time the brooding O'Hegarty listened carefully, but held his counsel. Finally he spoke – slowly, deliberately and incisively – as his officers remained silent. They knew not to interrupt him. He had concluded that it was impossible to hijack the *Upnor* within the harbour therefore they'd have to carry out an operation at sea. Sandow would lead the attack, while the main team would consist of Mick Murphy, Mick Leahy, Peter O'Donovan, Tom Crofts, Seán O'Donoghue and Con O'Sullivan. Jim Gray would be in charge of transport, Connie Neenan was to mobilise hundreds of volunteers in a support role and they'd need the help of Mick Burke.

O'Hegarty continued: 'The odds against us are 1,000 to one and even if we succeed you won't all make it back. You should think about it carefully and decide whether you're prepared to take the risks. If not you can withdraw without any reflection on your character or it being held against you.'

'However, if by some miracle we get our hands on this stuff, we can keep Collins and Mulcahy out of Cork. Then if the Free Staters or the British want to take us on let them try, but we'll slaughter the bastards'.

He reminded them that under no circumstances should anyone else be told about the plan, including other members of the brigade. They would need to enlist the help of a whole host of collaborators, some voluntary and some coerced, but no one was to know the objective or to be given an overview of the enterprise.

Seán asked everyone individually whether they were in or not. No one pulled out, but how could they without losing face? He then went over the details, assigned tasks and specified what they needed.

Dan 'Sandow' O'Donovan was the natural choice to command the operation, except that he had never been to sea before. He knew absolutely nothing about ships and the ocean; he hardly knew the bow from the stern, or the port from the starboard. But he was smart, resourceful and calm under fire; for him violence was necessary but he didn't revel in it. A carpenter by trade he was also a champion Gaelic Athletic Association (GAA) football player. With jet black hair, he was short in stature but stocky and athletic looking. He got his nickname from Eugen Sandow, the world famous German strongman, whose image was once plastered all over Cork on posters advertising Murphy's Stout and showing him hoisting a draft horse high above his head with one hand.

Sandow had led the squad that gunned down Lieutenant Colonel Gerald Smyth, Divisional Commissioner of the RIC, in 1920 as he sat in an armchair in the smoking room of the County Club in the centre of Cork. It was said – though most likely apocryphal – that before he emptied his revolver Sandow uttered: 'Colonel Smyth, you said to shoot [the IRA] on sight. Now, you are in sight and you are going to be shot!' He had led the brigade flying column, was second in command at the Coolnacaheragh ambush and more recently had kidnapped the journalist Arthur Kay.

Sandow's second in command, Mick Murphy was also a carpenter and was the captain of the Cork hurling team, going on to win three All-Ireland championships. He was a powerful good looking man, with a moustache and his hair beginning to turn grey. Murphy was above all a gunman – he wasn't as cerebral as some of his comrades such as Sandow and Tom Crofts. Commander of the 2nd Battalion, he led many daring attacks, including the Parnell Bridge attack on an RIC patrol in the centre of Cork. But above all, he had a reputation for eliminating numerous alleged spies and informers. Unlike the others in O'Hegarty's crowd Murphy was boastful with a tendency to embellish stories of his deeds, though that didn't make him any less lethal.

Obviously Mick Leahy was included on the team, given that he was a marine engineer and had already been involved in the attempt to bring in arms from Genoa.

Peter O'Donovan was the commander of the Active Service Unit, a group of a dozen or so full time fighters who were the brigade's elite fighting force within the city. Close to Murphy he had participated in several executions, most notably at Waterfall in November 1920, when three British army intelligence officers, dressed as civilians, were seen boarding a train. A small group of volunteers, including O'Donovan, led them from the train to a field, where they were shot and secretly buried. The following year having been captured and imprisoned in Victoria Barracks, he was badly beaten up.

Tom Crofts had never come across a job he wouldn't volunteer for; a former clerk with the Great Southern and Western Railway he was a long-standing member of both the IRB and IRA and highly regarded as a brigade officer.

In January 1921 when O'Hegarty and most of the leadership left for Ballyvourney he was put in charge of a newly formed city command, comprising the 1st and 2nd Battalions and with a total strength of 2,000. The RIC, who knew of Crofts by name but not by sight, placed him at the top of their 'murder list'. However, a few months later when he was captured after a shootout he gave his name as 'Tom Flavin', which saved him from being executed.

Despite being beaten in captivity at Victoria Barracks he refused to divulge any information and was eventually transferred to Spike Island. In November he and six other prisoners slipped out of their cell block at dusk, they hid in a disused tunnel built into the inner prison wall until darkness fell but before the searchlights were turned on. Avoiding the sentries they dashed across the dry moat, scaled the outer wall with an improvised rope ladder and with their hands protected by socks they cut the barbed wire at the top before making their descent. They then snuck down to the jetty and evading an army patrol managed to find a row boat and escaped to Queenstown.

Seán O'Donoghue – formerly a shop assistant – was best known for leading a revolver and hand grenade ambush at Dillon's Cross, a few hundred metres from Victoria Barracks, which resulted in the death of an Auxiliary and the wounding of eleven. This attack helped trigger the

Auxies subsequent burning of Cork city centre.

The final member of Sandow's team was Con 'Corney' O'Sullivan the brigade's senior engineering officer, who along with Sandow and Seán O'Donoghue had been involved in the killing of Lieut Col Smyth. He also fought with the column at Coolnacaheragh.

A week or so later O'Hegarty summoned Mick Burke to meet with him and Sandow. O'Hegarty brusquely instructed him to put together a ship's crew and keep them on standby. Burke was familiar with the harbour area and knew more about the sea than any of the others (aside from Leahy) and he told Sandow that they needed two things: the King's Harbour Master's official flag and a large manila envelope similar to those used for admiralty dispatches.

Burke returned to Queenstown where he had set up headquarters in the recently evacuated RIC barracks on West View and through an intermediary he made contact with De Courcy. Telling him to let him know when the *Upnor* was ready to sail and also to steal an envelope and the flag, the latter of which flew on a flagpole outside Capt. Usborne's office on East Beach. The enterprising De Courcy carried out his assignment and the items were soon on their way to Sandow, who was particularly chuffed to have in his possession an envelope embossed with the royal crown.

Next Burke met with John Duhig an IRA volunteer who lived in a house on Cottrell's Row in the Holy Ground. The forty-four year old Duhig was well respected for his knowledge of ships and seafaring, having reputedly served as a fitter – repairing marine engines – in Haulbowline during the war and was an experienced sailor. In the aftermath of the 1917 Bolshevik revolution he travelled to Russia and returned to Queenstown advocating for both a republican and a socialist revolution, in the tradition of James Connolly.

Although his belief in Marxism was unconventional, he was someone Burke knew he could depend on and Duhig agreed to help him assemble a crew of Royal Navy veterans who were either IRA volunteers or sympathisers. He could arrange to have four deckhands and two firemen (or stokers) ready to put to sea at a moment's notice. Burke didn't explain the details of the operation to Duhig and he didn't need to either.

By early March, the plans had been finalised. Sandow had his flag and envelope and he and Mick Leahy had completed their survey of the coastline. All the necessary equipment had either been procured or had been identified for hijacking. Jeremiah Collins – a merchant marine captain from the city – was chosen for a key role, though he was oblivious to the fact. Everyone and everything was in place and ready to go.

Given the brigade's ignorance of seafaring, the planning had been largely theoretical. But practicality didn't pose an obstacle to Sandow, who was long accustomed to using his imagination.

Any reasonable and rational commander would have dismissed the undertaking as foolhardy in the extreme. Not only was the underlying premise overly optimistic, but the project entailed an elaborate sequence of actions, each dependent on the other and should one component fail

129

then the whole operation would fail. But there was no other way for them to get the munitions needed to defend their 'republic'. Maybe their naivety and inexperience of operating at sea would prove to their advantage.

O'Hegarty and Sandow were unsure when the *Upnor* would actually set sail and in the meantime they had to wait until word came from De Courcy and that took a few more weeks.

10

The Ball at their Feet

In Cork city O'Hegarty and his brigade remained un-challenged, at least for now, but as Patrick McHugh, an anti-Treaty IRA officer from Dublin, realised: 'the Cork men were not at this time as keenly alive to the seriousness of the position; they had experienced no opposition and had the ball entirely at their own feet. The Free State headquarters [GHQ] had not spread its arm that far [yet]'.

In the meantime, the violence and disorder continued unabated. On 9 March, two – of the few remaining – RIC were walking down Hanover Street unarmed and in plain clothes, when they were confronted by a group of young men with revolvers. After the 'lads' shouted 'hands up' one of the constables managed to make a run for it amid a hail of bullets, while Dudley O'Sullivan, a native of Skibbereen, was fatally shot in the chest and left hip. Liam de Róiste lamented that the 'present disturbances including robberies and murders ... are the inevitable aftermath of the war period'.

Around the same time, Michael Collins decided to hold a rally in Cork. Though to avoid a confrontation with O'Hegarty he opted to go by train without an armed guard. The meeting was advertised as a 'Monster Treaty Demonstration' and set for Sunday 12 March. Special trains were laid on to bring in supporters from all over Cork.

The night before the two platforms on the Grand Parade were 'dismantled by a number of young men directed by a few women' and the timber beams along with banners were hurled into the River Lee. In their place, streamers with the word 'Surrendered' were hoisted on the tramway poles. While in the morning some of the trains heading into the city were stopped by armed men and their drivers taken away.

On Sunday morning, Collins and his entourage visited St Finbarr's cemetery to pay their respects at the Republican Plot where the martyrs of Cork 1 Brigade were buried, most notably the two ex-lord mayors, Terence MacSwiney and Tomás MacCurtain.

Tom Crofts and a dozen or so volunteers got there beforehand. With revolvers drawn they formed a cordon and in deadly earnest told him that they had orders to shoot if he dared 'put his foot inside' the plot. In the ensuing standoff Collins kept his cool, until he finally backed down and placed the wreath outside of the ropes. That the two IRA factions were fighting over the legacy of their dead was a measure of how deep and bitter the divide had become.

However, by the time Collins arrived at the Grand Parade the platforms had been rebuilt and a rapturous crowd of at least 50,000 greeted him. Two or three dozen IRA members had dispersed themselves among the throng, led by brigade officers, including Tom Crofts and most likely Sandow, Mick Murphy and Connie Neenan.

When Liam de Róiste spoke, the volunteers fired their revolvers into the air attempting to panic and disperse the throng. De Róiste paused for a moment and then said pointedly: 'We were not afraid of the Black and Tans and we are not afraid of them [O'Hegarty's crowd].'

Collins took the podium as 'hats and handkerchiefs were waved and drums were beating'. Someone shouted 'the hearts of the people are with you'. Standing with a folded newspaper casually jutting out of his jacket pocket, he leaned forward scanning the audience from side to side as he spoke; at times gesticulating into the air for emphasis. He passionately defended the Treaty for granting 'the right of the people of Ireland to rule themselves without interference from any outside power' and attacked de Valera who had spent most of the War of Independence safely in America. He justified the agreement as the inevitable price to pay for independence: 'If we had been able to beat the British out [of Ireland] … there need have been no negotiations … We had not beaten the enemy, but neither had he beaten us'.

Several other speakers followed and the interruptions steadily increased. There were shouts of 'we want a Republic' and at one stage a group started singing *The Boys of the First Cork Brigade*. The IRA attempted to storm the stage, but was held back by the crowd who formed a human chain. More shots were fired and 'little children screamed and some of them took refuge underneath the platform, while others were conveyed out of the crowd'. In the melee two of the volunteers were disarmed and a Franciscan priest was seen 'struggling with a man who had a revolver in his hand'. Remarkably there were no serious casualties.

With all the chaos, Seán O'Hegarty might well have

thought that he had scored a victory, but instead Collins' visit had highlighted the breadth and depth of support for the Treaty in the city.

In public Collins continued to present an assured and authoritative demeanour, but his many responsibilities combined with the relentless attacks from old friends and associates were taking their toll. Seán O'Hegarty's older brother, Patrick Sarsfield, who was a senior pro-Treaty Sinn Féin politician, saw that his friend 'Mick ... [was] tired out, irritable, overburdened with work and responsibility, some new worry every day and all the time brooding over the taunts that were freely thrown at him of being a traitor ... he was extremely sensitive on that point'.

But what struck De Róiste was that there was now an 'actual likelihood of Collins' being shot and killed by his former comrades.

Captain Jeremiah Collins was one of those who packed the platforms on the Grand Parade. An ardent admirer of Michael Collins he was no doubt horrified by the antics of O'Hegarty's volunteers. The sixty-eight year old master mariner was a wealthy shipper and coal importer. On the one hand, Capt. Collins was an Irish nationalist, on the other he was a member of the city's establishment, accustomed to working with the titled Anglo-Irish 'old money'. He was on the executive board of the radical United Irish League, but he was also a member of the Cork Harbour Commissioners and a patron of the Royal Cork Sailor's Home, a charity for Royal Navy veterans.

For much of his career his lifestyle was characteristic of

many prosperous nineteenth century home rulers. In 1912 when Winston Churchill visited Cork Harbour and met with the commissioners, Jeremiah greeted him, attired in a top hat, morning jacket and waistcoat with a watch chain across his chest – the embodiment of an English gentleman.

But around the time of the 1916 Rising his politics changed and – unusual for someone of his social standing – he went on to enthusiastically embrace the IRA's struggle. Eight years after he had welcomed Winston Churchill to Cork, he travelled to London with a Sinn Féin delegation to attend the requiem mass for Terence MacSwiney, this time inconspicuously dressed like an office clerk.

Though he was never a member of the IRA he provided invaluable support; often sheltering fugitives in his home and then whisking them on board one of his colliers to Liverpool. Amongst those he helped escape in the aftermath of the 1916 Rising was Liam Mellows, who later became the Director of Purchases at GHQ. Jeremiah Collins smuggled in weapons for Mellows so often that he was regarded as his agent in Cork. When Mick Murphy made a collection for an arms' fund he was surprised when the captain willingly donated – the considerable sum of – £150.

In 1921, the RIC requisitioned one of his steamers the *John Somers* for ferrying constables within the harbour. The wily Collins spotted a weakness in the contract and made a claim for the extraordinary fee of £3,608, 10s. and 4.d. His bill caused consternation within the RIC and the matter even found its way to the House of Commons, until Collins settled for a still generous £1,511.

With the signing of the Treaty, Capt. Collins had what he wanted. The country would be self-governing, but at the same time the leadership of the Free State could be trusted to provide political and economic stability and protect the rights of property owners like him. Alternatively, if Seán O'Hegarty and the anti-Treaty IRA were to gain the upper hand the country would be plunged into renewed war with little prospect of a functioning civil administration.

Collins and his family lived in an elegant three-storey, red-bricked Georgian house on South Terrace, a tree lined street south of the river. South Terrace was down the street from Jeremiah's offices and main warehouse on Buckingham Place and close to the quays where his ships off-loaded their coal. It was an easy walk to many of the major businesses in the city, including his bank on the South Mall, and his various social haunts. He also owned Carrigmahon a beautiful river front estate close to Queenstown, with its own riding stables and baths.

Given their longstanding involvement in the city's nationalist associations Jeremiah and Seán O'Hegarty had at least a passing acquaintance, however their personalities and politics were widely divergent and Jeremiah didn't have had any direct involvement with Cork 1 Brigade. But unknown to him, O'Hegarty had chosen him for the maritime adventure of his life.

Whereas 1922 was shaping up to be a good year for O'Hegarty and his brigade – with little prospect of the Free State forces gaining a toehold in the city – for Ernest Gaunt it was a different matter.

He complained that ever since Mick Burke – whom he thought was the head of the town's 'Free State Police' – had established himself in the RIC barracks, the 'police' consisted of 'young men in mufti [plain clothes] with no regular beats'. He noted that the harbour master's flag had recently been stolen in broad daylight and he felt it highly unlikely that Burke would make any effort of find the perpetrator.

With his command in Queenstown coming to an un-remarkable end he was 'rather depressed over his own pro-spects', worried that he'd soon be forced into retirement and that the government would renege on its promise of an Australian governorship. But there were several factors in his favour: the king remained a steadfast supporter and he enjoyed a sterling reputation for dependability and com-petency at the admiralty. In the meanwhile, he'd have to muddle through – after all that was the navy way.

By mid March the *Upnor* was fully laden, but there was still no word from De Courcy as to when she'd sail and O'Hegarty was forced to turn his attention to another pressing matter. Ever since January the anti-Treaty IRA, had been calling for the holding of an Army Convention to recognise the IRA as 'a sovereign independent body – not accountable to any civilian authority' – and thereby freeing itself from the oversight of the Dáil and its pro-Treaty majority. But at the last minute, Risteárd Mulcahy, under intense pressure from the Provisional Government, banned the convention.

Despite this, the meeting went ahead and on Sunday 26 March, over 200 delegates from all over the country converged on the Mansion House in Dublin. The agenda was of such crucial importance that even with the *Upnor* job imminent, O'Hegarty and his 'crowd' had to go and so he, Sandow, Mick Leahy, Mick Murphy, Tom Crofts, Connie Neenan and others set off for Dublin, prepared to make a speedy return should word reach them of any developments at Haulbowline.

They were wary of a confrontation with Michael Collins' forces and in Mick Leahy's words: 'we all went up prepared to fight ... in a hell of a big column'. Leading the way was one of the most extraordinary vehicles that has ever been seen in Ireland, the armoured car the *River Lee*. The *Lee* was originally a Crossley tender that Cork No. 1 captured from two Auxiliary intelligence officers, Agnew Bertram and Lionel Mitchell in November 1920 when the pair brought the lorry to the Johnson and Perrott garage for repair. Jim Gray, who was working there at the time, passed word onto his comrades and when the two cadets returned they were abducted at gunpoint, hauled off to Knockraha, interrogated and executed.

Gray hid the truck and eventually brought it to the Ford factory on the Marina where he oversaw its transformation. He got steel plates from armoured window shutters taken from evacuated RIC barracks. The truck body was then removed from the chassis and replaced by an enormous rectangular box made from the plates riveted together. In the front, there was a slit for the driver and on each side there were multiple gun loops. One volunteer remarked that this ungainly, slow-moving vehicle resembled a labourer's cottage on wheels.

When the brigade headed to the convention Jim Gray drove in front with the *River Lee*, flying a Tricolour and with a Lewis gun protruding out of one of the gun loops. It was like travelling in a metal box with the impact of every rut and pothole in the untarred road resonating throughout the contraption. What's more, there was no proper ventilation and it soon became insufferably hot and stuffy. Nevertheless with Jim at the wheel it proved to be faster than the remainder of the convoy and he was able to pull into several pubs along the way and still keep ahead. This continued until the abstemious O'Hegarty discovered that Gray was drunk and in his fury had him unceremoniously removed from the armoured car.

The Cork contingent caused quite a stir when they arrived at the Mansion House, carrying machine guns, Thompson guns, rifles, revolvers and grenades. They and the other delegates streamed into the Round Room where the Dáil had ratified the Treaty only a few months earlier. The mood was grim. They unanimously passed a motion: 'that the Army [IRA] reaffirms its allegiance to the Irish Republic ... [and that henceforth it should be under the control of] an Executive appointed by the convention'. But beyond that there was no consensus and the meeting was marked by considerable disorder, climactic speeches and calls to arms. There were moments of high drama, as when Tom Barry urged the overthrow of the Provisional Government, the establishment of a military dictatorship and the declaration of war against Britain. Seán O'Hegarty who 'was truly in fighting mood' was subsequently elected to the Army Executive.

The meeting only served to highlight the discord amongst the opponents of the Treaty and their inability to agree on a common strategy. There was little doubt that the country was hurtling down the road towards civil war.

The following day Seán O'Hegarty was in such a hurry to return that he couldn't even wait for a cup of tea before hitting the road. However, outside the village of Clogheen in Tipperary the *River Lee* broke down. It was getting dark and Joe Power (Gray's replacement as driver) worked on the engine by candle-light. He removed the dirty carburettor and was flushing it with petrol from a can, but failed to notice he was standing too close to the candle when all at once there was an almighty explosion. Everybody leaped out of the armoured car, taking with them machine guns, ammunition and the lot. Connie Neenan rushed to help Power, whose clothing was on fire, wrapping his overcoat around him and rolling him back and forth on the road to extinguish the flames.

With Power in considerable pain from burns to his face and hands, they were forced to rest for the night. As was so often the case a local family – this time it was the Brown's – took them in. According to Neenan: 'We received all the food and care we wanted, their hospitality knew no bounds and after we had all finished eating we sat around the fire – it being a rather nippy night – spiritedly discussing the happenings of the convention and then just chatting away amicably for the rest of the night'. All that is, except for Seán O'Hegarty, who was 'incensed about all this delay'. Neenan was amused by the irony of the situation: 'I could not help grinning to myself because, here we had been stuck for the whole night with nothing else to do but chat away and drink innumerate cups of tea', while earlier in Dublin Seán had been in too much of a rush to have a single cup.

Finally on Tuesday they arrived back in Cork; primed for action.

11

The *Warrior*

Tuesday, 28 March 1922

As the slightly singed *River Lee* was rumbling into Cork, Gen. Strickland was building a chicken run in his garden and Ernest Gaunt was busy at work at Haulbowline, while Lieut Leonard Williams, master of the tugboat *Warrior*, steamed out of Queenstown with *HMS Medusa* in tow. The *Medusa* was a rusty old hulk – decommissioned and stripped of her guns and fittings – that had recently been used as floating storage within the harbour. Although when she was launched in 1888, she was a gleaming state of the art cruiser, armed with torpedo tubes and six inch guns, and was swift enough to outrun most ships afloat. But now she was on her final voyage to the breaker's yard in England.

Williams was an experienced and highly skilled tugboat captain and this promised to be a routine trip. He knew the route well and since the weather was favourable with a gentle northerly breeze, he expected to arrive early the next day. The forty-nine year old Len was a Londoner through and through, but he had Irish roots. His father Robert – a watchmaker and a Baptist lay preacher – was born in Dublin and though he emigrated to England as a young man he was proud of his Irish heritage and remained an avid home ruler all his life.

Having serving his apprenticeship on the River Thames Len worked on small boats around Britain and even as far afield as Canada and Argentina. During the Great War, he was stationed at Queenstown as a Royal Navy reserve officer in command of the *Warrior*. From there, he rescued the passengers and crew of numerous torpedoed ships; frequently towing the disabled vessels back to port.

On 7 May 1915, he rushed to the aid of the *Lusitania* after she had been attacked by a submarine off the Old Head of Kinsale. Leonard and the *Warrior* brought ashore seventy-four passengers at Queenstown and the next day he went back, but this time to fish dead bodies out of the water. In all 1,195 out of 1,959 passengers and crew died, scores of them Americans in an event that shocked the citizens of Queenstown, Britain and America and helped propel the United States into the war.

After the war, Leonard developed post-traumatic stress disorder – or traumatic neurasthenia as it was then known, which was the officers' version of 'shell shock' – and was discharged from the navy. However, following hospital treatment and time spent recuperating at home in the company of his wife Ada, and their four children, he returned to sea by 1922; once more in command of the *Warrior* which was back under the control of its civilian owners the Elliott Steam Tug Company of London.

The *Warrior* was a tried and tested twenty-seven year old tug, just over thirty metres in length, she was originally built for working on the Thames. Like all tugs, she was relatively broad and short and lay low in the water. The superstructure painted brown topped her black steel hull. Behind her short main mast with its navigation and towing lights, was an open top bridge containing the ship's wheel, a brass binnacle encasing the compass to protect it from the elements and the engine order telegraph, which enabled Len to transmit his orders to the engine room. There was also a rope pull for operating the steam whistle. A waist high wooden parapet enclosed the wheelhouse, on either side of which was a pair of navigational lights: green on the starboard and red on the port.

On the deck below the bridge was the chartroom and just to the rear on the starboard side was a tiny narrow galley for the cook, John Gear, containing a coal burning stove, a counter and a bucket to wash up in. Aft of the bridge was a tall black, slightly raked funnel with the Elliott Company colours – a St George's Cross flag, in the centre of which were two towing hooks and a towrope. On the port side of the funnel was the lifeboat suspended between two davits.

The *Warrior's* engine was below decks and was powered by high-pressure steam generated by heating water in a boiler. To the fore was the boiler room containing a large cylindrical tank – almost five metres in diameter with a capacity of 33,000 litres of water – and beneath it the fireboxes for burning coal. Between the boiler and engine rooms there was a narrow passageway, with space for only one person to squeeze by, flanked on either side by huge bunkers capable of storing 100,000 kilograms of coal. The engine itself was a triple expansion engine, with three cylinders and pistons that operated at different steam pressures.

When the ship went to sea, the two stokers shovelled coal into the fireboxes, thereby heating the water in the boiler and creating the steam, which was piped aft to the engine. In the engine room, Lewis Hills, the first engineer, stood by the engine order telegraph and carried out Williams' commands. By turning a wheel valve he regulated the amount of steam released into the engine and hence the tugboat's speed. And by pulling the lever of the Stephenson valve, he could send the boat into reverse.

The crew's quarters took up relatively little room. In front of the boiler room was a small comfortable saloon with a cabin on either side, one for Capt. Williams and the other for Hills. Behind the engine was a spartan aft cabin tightly packed with narrow bunk beds for the remainder of the crew, with a stove in front and a little table in the centre. The aft cabin was accessed from the main deck by a companionway equipped with a narrow ladder.

Aside from Len Williams and Lewis Hills, the crew consisted of the Mate Charles Parker, Second Engineer William Adey, Able Seamen Charles Regan and Herbert Perrett, two stokers Henry Hurley and Henry Harris and the cook John Gear.

On that cloudy March afternoon Leonard and his crew sailed past the fortresses guarding the harbour entrance and set a course east towards England. Standing on the bridge he cut a dashing figure with his Royal Navy style beard, a double breasted navy jacket with two columns of brass buttons and his cap tilted a little to the side; 'at the Beatty angle' as he liked to say. His only challenge was his profound deafness;

the result of decades of working amidst the loud clashing and clanging of machinery.

However, beyond the harbour, the *Warrior* began to make less and less progress and by evening any hope Leonard had of arriving early the next day became increasingly doubtful. Although the wind shifted to the east creating a headwind, it still remained light and the main obstacle was the *Medusa* itself with its fouled bottom – the old hull being covered by a thick layer of barnacles, seaweed and algae from years of neglect – which in addition to the ship's already hefty 2,000 tons proved to be too much of a drag for the little tug.

Eventually after nightfall with the *Warrior* reduced to a speed of under four knots Leonard decided that the best course of action was to return to Queenstown and wait for more favourable conditions. Therefore, he turned around and headed back to Cork, expecting to get in the following morning.

12

A SPEEDY DEPARTURE

It all began at 9 a.m. when Mick Burke phoned the All for Ireland Club to tell Seán that De Courcy had informed him the *Upnor* was due to sail in about two hours. Everyone sprang into action; Sandow assembled his squad; Jim Gray retrieved the two motor cars he was keeping on standby at Johnson and Perrott Garage, which was conveniently located just across the street from the Club. Sandow's scouts reported that Jeremiah Collins had left his home and was heading towards the South Mall. And as he and Mick Murphy were about to leave to intercept the captain, Seán walked over; 'don't fuck up' he told them, which they knew was his way of saying 'look after yourself'. Sandow smiled to hide his uneasiness and said 'I'll see you later tonight, chief'.

Capt. Jeremiah Collins walked briskly along South Terrace, heading to his bank on the South Mall. After-wards he was due to attend a meeting of the Harbour Com-missioners in their stately boardroom at the Customs House. As always he looked looking extremely dapper; wearing a winter overcoat and bowler hat with a brown leather brief case in his left hand and walking stick in the other. It was a surprisingly brisk spring morning and in the cold air he could see the steam from his breath.

Despite carrying with him the considerable sum of £360 – over twice the annual salary of many of the city's workers – he failed to notice that he was being watched. In fact he had had been under surveillance for the past two weeks. This morning a young man with his cap pulled down – hands in his pockets and taking a drag on a cigarette in a futile attempt to stay warm – followed.

South Terrace merged into George's Quay and across the river was Holy Trinity church with its overly ornate Gothic spire and facade. He crossed Parliament Bridge and went up the narrow street before rounding the corner onto the South Mall, an elegant broad avenue that was the banking and professional centre of the city. All the while the young fellow remained twenty or so metres behind.

Suddenly there was a screech of brakes and a car abruptly pulled up alongside. Out jumped a man carrying a revolver, who opened the rear door and motioned for him to get in.

'Take my case, but don't shoot', implored Collins who was uncharacteristically frightened. 'Don't worry captain, just follow our instructions; you're in good hands', replied Sandow. Adding: 'There's someone in Cobh who wants your help with a job. Government work'. In the back Mick Murphy sat beside Jeremiah, with his Thompson gun lying innocently on the floor.

This was not the first tight spot Collins had been in and he soon regained his composure and asked his kidnappers to let him deposit his money at the bank. With Sandow covering him, a revolver concealed under his coat, Jeremiah lodged the cash and they were soon off on their way to Cobh.

They sped up Pembroke Street, past the post office, onto St Patrick's Street, with its burned out shops and businesses, across St Patrick's Bridge spanning the north channel of the River Lee, right onto MacCurtain Street – which two years earlier the Sinn Féin led city council had renamed from the original King Street – and out the Glanmire Road past the low red brick railway station. Above them on the hill was the once feared Victoria Barracks.

On the outskirts of the city, the broad expanse of the River Lee opened up on their right, bordered by the tree lined Marina, further along the estates of gentry and wealthy merchants – largely hidden amongst groves of deciduous trees – dotted the hillside to the left. A few minutes later they were in the countryside and surrounded by the tillage fields and lush pastureland of east Cork with its rolling hills; before the village of Carrigtwohill they took a right turn and passed Fota House, the enormous estate of Lord Barrymore. Following that they crossed the sturdy stone arched bridge at Belvelly with a fifteenth century tower house on their left. They were now on the Great Island and closing in on Cobh.

The road ran parallel to the estuary of the River Lee; they drove by Rushbrooke dockyards while across the channel Capt. Collins' glimpsed his Carrigmahon mansion surrounded by woodlands. Then up the hill past fine houses on the eastern outskirts of the town. The road curved down a steep gradient affording magnificent views of Haulbowline and Spike Islands and then onto Westbourne Place where they slowed to take the hairpin bend opposite the Royal Cork Yacht Club and finally down to the train station – the busiest little station in

Ireland and the last stop for hundreds of thousands of Irish emigrants on their way to America – at the water's edge.

Forty minutes after leaving the South Mall they arrived at the Deepwater Quay where they were to rendezvous with Mick Burke and to seize the tug *Hellespont*. Having dropped them off, the driver spun around and headed towards Midleton to pick up Mick Leahy.

Back in Cork, Jim Gray and his brother Miah got the red Buick ready for the rest of the party; this was his pride and joy, a beautiful sleek seven seater, six cylinder open tourer. This was the car which he had once fearlessly accelerated in an attempt to clear a partly demolished bridge, ejecting and almost killing Tom Barry. He had cut a rectangular opening in the windscreen on the passenger side for a forward facing Lewis gun. The engine had recently been overhauled and the tyres were brand new, all courtesy of Johnson and Perrott; not that they had any say in the matter.

The brothers topped up the radiator with water. They strapped several two gallon cans of petrol onto the running boards and stowed a can of oil and one of water along with spare parts on board. Next came two jute sacks, one with a Lewis gun and the other with a Thompson gun and then the ammunition. Finally, they placed the Harbour Master's flag and the manila envelope carefully in the back.

Tom Crofts, Peter O'Donovan, Seán O'Donoghue and Con O'Sullivan together with Leo Buckley climbed on board. They were dressed like 'real Shinners': all wore caps, under their long coats they had leather Sam Browne belts with a shoulder strap and a .45 service revolver at each hip. Everyone had army style leggings. With that, they were off on a mad dash to Cobh, soon arriving at the Deepwater Quay. They hopped out of the car while Leo Buckley remained for the one hour drive to Roches Point.

The four walked over to the side of the train station where Sandow and Murphy had been joined by Mick Burke, John Duhig and his crew. 'Everything's in order', Burke confidently told them. From experience, he knew that there was always a suitable vessel at the quay which they'd be able to seize. And sure enough the *Hellespont* was steaming towards them. Seeing the tugboat made Sandow queasy: 'None of us had been at sea before and we had more qualms about setting out in the ocean in this cockleshell … than we had over meeting the combined British army and navy'.

However, to their horror the *Hellespont* sailed past, continuing on in the direction of Monkstown. The normally unflappable Sandow was livid and turned to Mick Burke. 'Jaysus Christ Mick I should never have listened to you. There's fuck all we can do now', though he was just as angry with himself for having accepted Burke's repeated assurances.

A volunteer ran along the shore, but returned dejected to say that the boat had gone in for repairs. At the same time, Burke was unable to locate any of the other tugs which were usually in the harbour. With nothing about to happen Capt. Collins was escorted under guard to the Rob Roy Hotel where he waited in the lounge drinking whiskey.

From where Sandow and his team stood, they had an unobstructed view of Haulbowline and the *Upnor*, just a few hundred metres away. At one o'clock the ship gave two long blasts of her horn, cast off her moorings and embarked for Devonport docks at Plymouth, 350 kilometres away. The usually sanguine Mick Murphy admitted he 'glared helplessly' at the sight. And if that wasn't bad enough, the driver returned from Midleton to report that Mick Leahy was nowhere to be found.

It looked like the game was up. The *Upnor* had safely left. They had no prospect of capturing the *Hellespont* or any other similar vessel. And without Leahy, they were missing a key player. But Sandow and his comrades weren't accustomed to quitting.

Eventually a docker told them that there was another tug, the *Flying Foam*, two kilometres away at Rushbrooke. Sandow and Mick Murphy set off, with Murphy carrying a Thompson under his coat.

As they were hurrying down Westbourne Place an elderly lady dressed in a traditional Cork shawl grabbed Mick excitedly by the elbow, exclaiming: 'God bless you and aren't you Mrs Murphy's boy?' He stiffened at the thought of being recognised and continued on, while much to Sandow's amusement she shouted after him: ''Tis you that has grown to be a fine man, God bless you. Sure I remember you when you were only a little nipper.' 'Mrs Murphy's little boy' simpered Sandow, to which Murphy responded with a murderous scowl.

They hadn't gone far when a runner caught up with them with the news that a tugboat had berthed at the Deepwater Quay.

The *Warrior* had left on Tuesday in good weather bound

for England and so her return the next day was unexpected. Len Williams – oblivious to the drama unfolding ashore – towed the *Medusa* to her mooring at Monkstown and then turned around and tied up at the Deepwater Quay. Within minutes of arriving, he disembarked and strode into town to meet with Andrew Horne, the local shipping agent for the Elliot Steam Tug Company and await further instructions.

Shortly afterwards Sandow and Murphy returned and they and the others walked up the tug's gangplank. The Mate Charles Parker came over and after Sandow asked to hire the boat, he told him to speak to Williams who had gone to see the agent 'near the clock tower'.

Sandow knew that if he seized the *Warrior* there and then and put to sea, when Williams returned and found his ship missing he'd be sure to raise the alarm. The navy would then dispatch a destroyer, which would easily overtake and corner the tug. Therefore, taking Burke and another Cobh volunteer, he set off to find Williams.

The *Warrior*'s crew must have been suspicious of the IRA party, particularly when some of them remained on board after Sandow left. But these were strange times in Cork and it was often better not to ask too many questions so they went back to their routine. Having just eaten lunch, Parker and three of the others went to the aft cabin for an afternoon nap. An able seamen and a stoker stayed on deck relaxing and having a chat and the cook, John Gear, was busy in the galley cleaning up. Lewis Hills returned to the engine room, checking that everything was in order, particularly after the difficulty the *Warrior* had run into on her tow of the *Medusa* and afterwards he went up on the bridge.

Sandow and Burke hurried along the seafront accompanied by the noise of squawking seagulls and the strong smell of seaweed. They passed the naval pier and its unsuspecting Royal Marine guard and the promenade with its Victorian bandstand; where in more peaceful times the army and Royal Marine bands used to give evening concerts. Then after the Cunard and White Star Line's offices they arrived at the harbour master's office with its bare flagpole.

For what felt like an eternity to Sandow, they searched all over for Williams; going in and out of offices, bars and hotels and asking anyone they met. A passerby pointed them in the direction of Lynch's Quay. There beyond the Customs House was a non-descript building at the beginning of a terrace with a sign announcing 'A. C Horne and Company, Steamship Brokers' and below that 'Lloyd's Agents'.

Andrew Coutts Horne, a Queenstown native and staunch unionist, was a well-respected businessman who had prospered through a combination of hard work, savviness and an aptitude for self-promotion. The fifty-one year old Horne – with an upturned handlebar moustache in the imperial style and a pronounced receding forehead – was in addition to being a shipping agent, the local consul for Belgium, Italy and Sweden; before the war he had also been consul for Germany and Austro-Hungry, but that was better forgotten. Gaunt's predecessor during the Great War, Admiral Lewis Bayly, said: 'Mr A C Horne, shipping agent, was always at hand. He represented so many shipping lines and his energy, with no fear of responsibility, enabled me to act quickly when survivors were brought in and had to be looked after at once. I shall always be grateful to Mr Horne for the way he facilitated matters'.

Sandow walked straight through to Horne's private office in the back, interrupting him and Capt. Williams and in a direct, but not unduly rude manner addressed Williams: 'We would like to charter your tug, captain. We want her for urgent government business'.

'Eh? What's that?' replied the deaf Williams cupping his hand around his ear.

Sandow raised his voice and repeated his request.

Williams and Horne both stared curiously at Sandow until the captain asked: 'We would have to know what you want her for?'

'Secret business' replied Sandow who paused and leaned towards them, adding 'but if I may speak confidentially' – the two men nodded – 'we want the tug immediately to transport government troops from Dungarvan to Cobh'.

'Why can't you send them by train?' inquired Williams.

Sandow shouted 'Out of the question, they'd be ambushed'. Williams suggested they telegraph the request to the Elliott Company and that they'd have the answer within two hours. The captain could see the distinctive bulge of revolvers inside the intruders' coats and he breathed a sigh of relief when they finally left.

However a few minutes later Sandow and his companions returned. This time they got straight down to business. Horne's phone rang and as he went to pick it up Sandow warned him not to say anything or he'd put a bullet through his head. Williams was then escorted to the Clyde Shipping Company office a few doors down, where he was guarded by two volunteers until he was transferred to the Rob Roy Hotel in the evening.

Burke bluntly told Horne that they'd decided not to kill him and that he was free to go, provided he'd give his word that he wouldn't mention anything about what had happened for another twenty-four hours. Horne, knowing that Burke could and would track him down, shook hands in agreement. And with that, Sandow and Burke headed back to the *Warrior*, stopping along the way to collect Capt. Collins at the Rob Roy.

Arriving at the quay they marched up the gangway and joined the rest of the IRA team on board. There was a scurry of activity. Three of the boarding party opened the hatchway to the aft cabin and slid down the narrow ladder into the space where Parker and three of the crew were sleeping, waking them with revolvers drawn. William Adey opened his eyes to see a gun under his nose. 'Don't move or you know what we usually do' they were told. There was no resistance.

The stoker and deck hand who were sitting up on deck were brought down to join their crewmates. On the bridge Hills, when he saw the armed men board, considered making a run down the gangway to the safety of the quay, but decided that he was unlikely to make it. 'Who's the engineer?' asked one of the intruders in the aft cabin. 'He's not here', replied Henry Harris a stoker who was sent back up to get Hills.

Afterwards the crew were led to the foredeck below the

bridge where Sandow told them that he had arranged with Leonard Williams to charter the *Warrior* for 'a secret mission' on behalf of the Provisional Government. Once Williams returned in another half an hour or so they'd set sail and he expected them to be gone no more than five hours.

However, as soon as Sandow verified with Parker that everyone was assembled on deck, he told them that they were all under arrest. Adding that as long as they cooperated he'd guarantee their safety. With that Hills was sent to the engine room accompanied by an armed guard, John Gear was consigned to the galley and the remainder of the crew returned to their cabin with three guards standing above the companionway. Sandow had the Lewis gun carefully stowed in the chart room.

Duhig's IRA crew came up the gangway carrying equipment and supplies. One of them brought with him his old Royal Navy woollen jersey. Another handed a heavy sack to Gear, saying: 'look after that with your life'. They 'were real tough old lads' accustomed to going to sea for months on end, some called them the Holy Grounders from where they hailed from.

Sandow walked over to Duhig: 'Are you sure you can sail this thing without Leahy?'

'I have to, don't I, commandant', replied Duhig. 'I've sent the engineer below to help out, but you'll have to keep an eye on him. Make sure he doesn't sabotage the bloody thing'. Duhig and his two stokers went down the ladder while the four deckhands took up position by the mooring ropes, ready to cast off.

Jeremiah Collins joined Sandow on the bridge, where he was told to set a course for Dungarvan. Collins didn't believe for a moment Sandow's explanation that they were going there to assist the Provisional Government, it was obvious to him that they were part of O'Hegarty's outfit, engaged in some sort of a rogue operation. But having helped out the IRA many times before he was prepared to cooperate – at least for now.

Having waited a few minutes to allow the stokers to shovel enough coal into the fireboxes and build up sufficient pressure in the boiler, Collins' reached for the engine order telegraph, turning the dial to 'full steam ahead'. Duhig acknowledged the command and opened the wheel valve releasing the steam to power the engine. 'You probably don't want me to blow the whistle' Collins said to Sandow with a smile.

They sailed parallel to the front of the town – recreating Sandow and Burke's walk to Horne's office, albeit with a better view. St Colman's cathedral and Admiralty House, both of which had been hidden when they were at the quay, soon came into view. Having passed inside of Spike Island they reached Spitbank Lighthouse – an engineering marvel that resembled a giant metal spider rising up from the seabed – where they slowed down to make a ninety degree turn and then headed straight for the harbour mouth.

As they approached the fortresses Jeremiah Collins turned to Sandow: 'Bunch of landlubbers! What type of a dummy captain do you think I am with a bowler hat on?' and pointing to the forts with their menacing guns said, 'What'd they think?' He snatched Sandow's cap for himself and instead placed the bowler on Sandow, amusing Sandow no end, especially when he found the hat to be a good fit.

The *Warrior* headed towards the steeply sloped promontories close to the entrance, with Forts Carlisle and Camden built on top of and tunnelled into the sandstone and surrounded by fields of coarse grass and gorse. She passed directly below the gun batteries, while straight behind was Fort Westmoreland. There was now enough firepower pointed at her to sink a fleet of battleships. But the tugboat was a familiar sight and despite her abrupt and unorthodox departure, she sailed safely through.

A little beyond was Fort Templebreedy on the right and to the left Roches Point with the lighthouse and the coastguard station, the latter of which had been captured earlier by Leo Buckley and three local volunteers. Then the *Warrior* was into the open ocean.

Sandow and his team were amazed that they had got so far, but their mood was considerably dampened when they found that the *Upnor* was nowhere to be seen. She had already a head start of two hours and it seemed unlikely that they'd ever find her. To come upon a ship in this vast expanse of grey water would be about as likely as finding a needle in a haystack.

13

THE BALLYCOTTON CONVOY

After Sandow and the others had left for Queenstown, Jim Gray went back to the task of assembling the transport needed for the job. It was a huge undertaking – the logistics of which was far beyond anything he or anyone else in the IRA had ever attempted before – but if anyone could pull it off, he could.

Gray, unlike the rest of O'Hegarty's inner circle, had joined the volunteers late in the game. He was 'discovered' working in a city garage alongside his father, who was an ex-British soldier. And although the brigade was initially wary of him because of his background, they desperately needed his expertise both as a mechanic and a driver. In those days 'driving was still a rare skill' and given the dreadful quality of the roads combined with the unreliability of cars and lorries, it was important for a driver to have mechanical know how. He quickly proved his worth.

With the title of brigade transport officer he became the go-to person whenever a car was needed for a job. If an ambush or shooting was planned outside of the city or someone needed to move a consignment of rifles, Jim could always be depended on to have a vehicle ready and waiting. In this he partnered with his older brother Jeremiah ('Miah').

He was fearless to the point of being foolhardy, possessing a total disregard for rules and conventions. Though at times ruthless, he could also be charming, fun and good natured. Seán Murray, the brigade's training officer, said: 'I have seen Jim blind drunk at the wheel, he would be able to drive once he had his hands on the wheel ... He was an awful mad man and he had no fear'.

Seán O'Hegarty helped the brothers open a garage in Summerhill – down the road from Victoria Barracks and close to the Black and Tan's headquarters at Empress Place – as a front for their IRA activities. There they got work from army officers and well-to-do locals.

Jim, posing as a loyalist, brazenly applied for permission to carry a revolver, on the pretext of needing it to protect himself and his business. District Inspector Oswald Swanzy of the RIC issued the permit and Gray afterwards passed on his 'legal' revolver to Tomás MacCurtain. In a bizarre turn of events MacCurtain was assassinated a few months later, by an RIC squad allegedly led by Swanzy, with the result that the IRA pursued him until eventually gunning him down with the very same weapon in Lisburn, County Antrim.

The Grays were accustomed to 'borrowing' customers' cars for jobs, until they decided that the brigade needed its own vehicle. As soon as they got a docket to repair an army lorry the pair went up the hill to Victoria Barracks, where they collected the lorry and then surreptitiously hitched a Ford van to it. Driving up to the main gate, they showed the sentry their paperwork for the lorry and calmly drove away with the stolen van in tow. Back at the garage, they stripped the van, got a battered car body from a dump and attached it to the chassis and that became the brigade's first motor car.

In March 1921 when Jim was with the column in Ballyvourney, O'Hegarty sent him and Sandow to Cork on a mission to kill Gen. Strickland. Along with three other volunteers, they set off in the red Buick and arriving in the city early in the morning, they coolly drove through the centre with a Lewis gun pointing out the windscreen and their rifles clearly visible. Resembling an Auxiliary patrol in civvies they passed groups of soldiers, who took little notice. When they approached Catfort Barracks 'the Black and Tan sentry at the gate saluted us smartly and we returned the salute'.

The attack on Strickland however was called off after he abruptly changed his plans. When they returned to the safety of Ballyvourney at nightfall Gray turned to his companions saying: 'we are as safe lads as if we were in God's pocket'.

As the fighting escalated, the brigade's appetite for vehicles became insatiable and the Grays adapted to meet the demand. According to John Borgonovo: 'The Gray brothers trained new drivers and identified the locations of cars, vans and lorries for quick seizure. In 1920 vehicle owners typically parked in private garages rather than on the street, so the Gray's secured keys to various garages, which became their own private motor pool. Throughout 1920 vehicle thefts in Cork frequently preceded IRA abductions or barrack assaults. IRA street fighters in Cork were sometimes mobile, throwing grenades from moving vehicles and firing machine guns from cars and motor-cycle sidecars. The volunteers often returned the vehicles when finished or told the owners where they could be found. By 1921, the brigade secured a few of their own cars, stolen from the city's wealthier citizens. The brigade also stockpiled tires, car parts, hundreds of gallons of stolen petrol and motorcycles'.

In the attack on Blarney RIC barracks in 1920 Jim and Miah seized up to a dozen cars and vans to bring the volunteers out from the city. But the *Upnor* job was to be much, much bigger. Jim was intent on getting every lorry and van he could lay his hands on, while Connie Neenan readied 2-300 volunteers in support. Jim drew up a list of the whereabouts of all the lorries he could find and one or two weeks before the operation he passed it onto Neenan, who divided his force into small groups and tasked them with keeping a watch on businesses and warehouses throughout the city. The volunteers waited for their final orders; they knew that there was a 'big job' planned, but Neenan gave them no information as to what it was and it wasn't until the day itself that they were told where they were going.

Finally on Wednesday a little before midday Neenan gave the go ahead. Volunteers armed with revolvers fanned out across the city. Delivery men and van drivers were approached by young men, who hopped into the cab and told them to drive to Ballycotton, a fishing village to the south-east. It was rarely necessary for them to brandish their weapons.

Within an hour or two, the vehicles were converging on Glanmire – beyond Victoria Barracks – where Gray and Neenan formed them into a convoy. In all there were seventy-seven lorries, six steam lorries, several cars and motor bikes and 'legend has it' a steam roller! It was a huge motley collection.

The trucks and vans were colourfully painted and carried the names of every conceivable merchant in Cork. There was a Ford van from Crosse and Blackwell Provision Merchants and Jam Makers and another from Lyons and Company Manufacturers of Ladies Underclothing. Together with lorries from O'Sullivan Furniture Removers, Cade and Sons Wine and Spirit Merchants, MacNaughton Building Materials and the Cork Steamship Company. Several large flatbed lorries had been commandeered from Murphy's Brewery – 'suppliers of stout to his Majesty's forces' – at Lady's Well, on the north side of the city.

Even in a city long accustomed to the unexpected, the sight elicited considerable interest. One newspaper wrote: 'The public was mystified by the sudden commandeering and subsequent departure from the city of a long train of one hundred motor cars and lorries'. The *Cork Constitution* in stilted prose reported: 'This ostentatious display it was that set [*sic*] speculation very actively in motion. Various and contradictory were the explanations and suggestions as to what new movements the political wind was taking. The explanation that met with most general acceptance was that an American ship, containing arms and ammunition for Young Ireland, had been signalled and was hovering off the southern coast waiting for connection with a transport service.'

But as usual, Liam de Róiste had his finger on the pulse: 'The "Irregulars" of Cork commandeered a large number of motor lorries of Cork merchants today. Captain Collins, who ran in some ships with arms previously, was also "commandeered", so it is surmised that "gun running" is taking place; off the coast of Waterford probably … With all the different armed forces and armed men, who are termed "Bolsheviks" in Cork, the prospect is indeed bleak for poor Ireland. The stage is being set for the civil war of blood … with the English as good "lookers-on".'

Jim Gray was satisfied with his work and his sole regret being that he couldn't take along the *River Lee*, which was far too big and heavy for the roads they were about to travel on. Since his relationship with O'Hegarty had temporarily soured after he was caught driving drunk on the way up to Dublin, the pair may have travelled in different cars. In contrast to Jim's optimism Seán was more realistic, knowing that they had a long and eventful day and night ahead.

As they thundered through village after village people must have been flabbergasted when they looked out of their homes. Their windows shook and floors vibrated; the streets were shrouded in a thick layer of dust mixed with the strong smell of exhaust. Most impressive of all were the powerful steam lorries built for hauling freight; belching clouds of smoke from their tall chimneys, they were literally steam engines on wheels powered by burning coal. They were mechanical monsters with large clunky metal fittings, huge wheels with solid rubber tires and the drivers sitting in their cabs high above the road. The cavalcade – travelling at less than twenty kilometres an hour – stretched on and on for at least two kilometres. It was not just the biggest convoy ever assembled in Cork and probably in all of Ireland, but it was the most fantastical sight ever seen in those parts.

However it was dangerously vulnerable to attack. Gen. Strickland had surely got wind of the hijackings and all he had to do was dispatch a mobile force supported by armoured cars, outflank the convoy, disable one or two of the leading lorries, thereby blocking the road and putting an end to the escapade. But true to form, O'Hegarty had planned for this and after the lorries passed Glanmire, work parties of IRA volunteers and local labourers blocked the roads. The *Constitution* reported: 'In the wake of the lorry cavalcade heavy trees had been felled across the Cork-Youghal road. It was argued that those engaged in such a mission would not thus have obstructed their own means of returning … It is however probable that its purpose was to prevent pursuit and interference in the event of information reaching the Crown forces'.

Sixteen kilometres beyond Cork they drove through Carrigtwohill, passing the burned out shell of the RIC barracks – half the roof and walls had collapsed into a heap of rubble and the second storey was missing its floor – two years after the attack led by Mick Leahy. Speaking of Leahy – who had been 'missing' earlier in the morning – it's likely that another car was sent to fetch him as they passed close to his home.

After several kilometres they crossed the Owenacurra River and then made a right turn down the main street of Midleton. A prosperous market town, famous for its whiskey distillery, it was also enemy territory and the town's

IRA was the only unit of Cork 1 to ally themselves with the Provisional Government. No doubt the lumbering procession was watched from behind squinting windows, but there was no time to mobilise and obstruct its progress.

At the end of the street, they took the road south for Ballycotton. They were entering the heart of the countryside. The road became narrow and windy and the surface was increasingly muddy, rutted and potholed. The largest craters had been crudely patched with stones, that presented yet another hazard. Tall unkempt hedgerows lined the sides and every now and again large deciduous branches formed a natural canopy overhead. They passed cottages and small farmyards, with their busy hens and barking dogs. The vehicles laboured on the hills and the going became increasingly difficult.

After a long climb the road gradually descended into the historic town of Cloyne, overlooked by an ancient round tower, clad in ivy and long since missing its conical roof. In the centre were the ruins of the fortified RIC barracks, which also had been captured and burned by Mick Leahy. They were just ten kilometres from Ballycotton.

It's uncertain what route they took after Cloyne. If they continued on straight through the town it would have been a difficult drive, up over the windswept hills. Whereas if they turned to the left towards Shangarry and the sea, the road was better, straighter and flatter. However, whatever way they went, they headed towards Ballycotton and then one or two kilometres before the village O'Hegarty ordered a halt.

The convoy came to a stop in the middle of the road,

which was far too narrow to allow them to pull over to the side. Everybody got out, stretched their legs and shared their 'meagre rations of bread and cigarettes'. There was a buzz of anticipation and excitement since by now there could have had no doubt that they were part of an operation to smuggle in weapons.

Sandow and Mick Leahy had earlier selected Ballycotton. The small isolated village was only twenty kilometres by sea from Roches Point, but forty kilometres by road from either Cork or Queenstown and any British forces wanting to get there would have had to drive along country byroads which were easily obstructed and where they were liable to get lost.

The picturesque village consisted of shops and pubs, a post office and churches as well as an RIC barracks and a coastguard station, both of which had been recently evacuated. There was the Bayview Hotel which invited visitors to enjoy the benefits of the fresh Atlantic air and it was said that 'doctors of repute prescribed a week in Ballycotton for patients suffering from fatigue', while the famous Cork politician William O'Brien declared 'it is one of the very sufficient consolations of a dying day to know that they are a breed as wholesome and stimulating as the ocean breezes that give Ballycotton its fame with the doctors'. The focal point of the village however was the pier, which was primarily used by fishing boats, but occasionally by merchants importing coal from England and sightseeing boats from Cork.

It was already late in the afternoon and Seán sent a car with a group of volunteers with orders to head straight to the pier. Meanwhile, he put the finishing touches to his elaborate plan to obstruct communications. His objectives were threefold: to prevent army units from approaching either from Cork to the west or Youghal to the east, to completely isolate Ballycotton and its inhabitants and to restrict and control Admiral Gaunt's communications out of Queenstown.

IRA units had already blocked the roads out of Cork and Youghal, both of which still had army garrisons. As soon as the convoy was approaching Ballycotton groups of volunteers and locals were busy severing the surrounding roads. It was tough work with axes, saws and shovels and they didn't finish until there was only one – unmarked – route in and out of the locality. Meanwhile others cut the telephone and telegraph wires, while an armed volunteer installed himself in the telephone exchange at the post office. There was now no way for anyone from Ballycotton to send a warning to the army in Cork.

The wires between Queenstown and Cork were severed so that Ernest Gaunt couldn't request help from Gen. Strickland. Finally Leo Buckley at Roches Point Coastguard Station controlled the base's telegraph instrument. Buckley was a trained telegraphist who during the War of Independence used his job at the post office to intercept the military's secret encrypted messages. Later he commanded the brigade's 'T Station' a hidden dugout built into a railway embankment and staffed round the clock by a team of eight volunteers. From there he was able to tap 'all the main telephone lines into and out from Cork city' by running wires from a nearby telephone pole into the hideout. According to him: 'All military and police conversations were listened to … If information of importance was picked up it was immediately sent to Brigade headquarters'. Now his job was to monitor messages sent by Ernest Gaunt, including secret coded ones to the admiralty in London, and block them if they appeared to be anything other than routine.

The *Irish Times* reported: 'Telegraphic and telephonic communications between Queenstown and Cork and other places was suspended this morning owing to wires having been cut and vehicular traffic on the main road leading to Cork was blocked at various points by means of felled trees.'

At the side of the road Seán waited anxiously for news of Sandow and his crew. He had seen his hopes dashed many times before and he had often meticulously planned an operation only for the whole thing to collapse due to some unforeseen hitch. There was the botched attack on Blarney RIC barracks, multiple unsuccessful efforts to kill or kidnap Strickland and several failed attempts to wipe out the Auxiliary division stationed in Macroom. Never mind the disastrous plan to smuggle in weapons from Italy, although in his mind Collins was to blame for that.

With this operation, there was simply too much that could go wrong and unknown to him had already gone wrong.

14

MESSAGE FROM THE ADMIRALTY

As soon as the *Warrior* passed Roches Point and was beyond the reach of the British guns Mick Burke and Mick Murphy joined Sandow and Jeremiah Collins on the bridge. Sandow and Murphy both took turns peering through a pair of binoculars, but no matter how hard or how long they looked there was no sign of the *Upnor*. At the same time, Burke instructed Capt. Collins to change their north-easterly course for Dungarvan to south-east for Plymouth.

But Sandow and his team didn't have a clue what to do next; to sail in the general direction of Plymouth was one thing, but to locate the arms ship before nightfall was a challenge far beyond their capabilities. Somehow they needed to determine the precise route taken by the *Upnor* and then plot a course to catch up with her. Meanwhile an increasingly exasperated Collins – long accustomed to being his own boss – found himself in the unfathomable situation of being ordered about by a pair of carpenters and a grocer's assistant. Eventually he turned to them: 'Would you lads mind telling me where we're supposed to be going?'

To which Murphy replied: 'That's if we can at this stage'.

Collins responded: 'If you don't explain to me what you're up to I can't help; the only thing I know for certain is that you're not on a secret mission to help Mick Collins'.

Reluctantly they were forced to accept that the elderly

captain was their last remaining hope; with decades of seagoing experience combined with a sharp intellect, he knew the sea lanes from Cork to England better than almost anyone else. And so they told him about their plan to seize the *Upnor*. Collins' reaction caught them off guard, in the words of Murphy, he was 'game to the gills'. He loved an adventure – after all wasn't he an accomplished arms smuggler himself – and he knew he was the right person for the job.

Sandow and Murphy accompanied Collins down the ladder and into the chartroom. The captain unfolded the little wooden drop leaf table and spread out an admiralty chart. 'We're sailing at twelve knots, but a fully loaded store ship like the *Upnor* has a cruising speed of nine knots. Therefore provided I can correctly estimate her bearings we can still intercept her.' Collins knew that on leaving the harbour the *Upnor* would have kept a southerly course for several kilometres before adjusting to a south-eastern direction towards the south-west tip of England. With a pencil and a navigation plotter, he carefully drew a triangle on the chart. Then, pointing with the pencil for emphasis, he stated: 'if we modify our present course a few degrees to the south south-east we can cut her off this evening at 6:30, but if we continue straight to Plymouth, as we're doing, we won't sight her until six tomorrow morning and by that time she'll be already off the south coast of England.'

Sandow mulled it over and with no other options, brusquely gave his consent. Thereupon Collins returned to the bridge and set course. Determined to find his quarry he drove the *Warrior* at full speed with smoke belching from her funnel and generating a large foaming bow wave. Although the weather remained cloudy, fortunately the sea was unusually calm and by late afternoon the wind dropped all the way down to Force 1.

Meanwhile Sandow gave the *Warrior's* crew – packed like sardines in the aft cabin – permission to come up on deck and get some fresh air. The atmosphere on board became incongruously relaxed; groups sat around chatting and smoking. The crew were relieved that their hijackers were obviously experienced and professional and so long as they abided by their instructions, they were likely to be safe. There were twenty-three crowded aboard the little tug.

Aside from the two IRA stokers toiling in the boiler room the hardest working person was John Gear, who emptied the heavy sack (which Duhig's men had given him) on the counter and went to work. 'I was kept in the galley all the time frying eggs and bacon and making tea for them', he complained. Meanwhile Collins stayed up on the freezing cold and unprotected wheelhouse.

The horizon remained clearly delineated and uninterrupted until around six o'clock – just as Collins had predicted – someone shouted: 'There she is!' Sandow came up the ladder to the captain, who pointed out a dark speck in the distance and above it a smudge of smoke. Even with the binoculars, it was impossible to make out any details but Collins was confident that this was the *Upnor*.

Gradually the ship's distinctive long profile came into view, with her two short masts and derrick, while aft was the bridge and a single funnel. She lay low in the water from her heavy cargo. Their expectations were confirmed when they spotted the naval ordnance ensign – a navy blue flag, with the union jack in the upper left corner, below that an anchor and to the right three canons in a column surrounded by a rope motif – flying from the stern.

It was approaching sunset and in the fading light Sandow and his comrades got a nasty shock when they thought they saw the *Upnor* had a naval escort. Fortunately for them, they soon realised that the other two ships merely happened to be sailing ahead on the same route. This was not the first time that they were beneficiaries of Ernest Gaunt's ineptitude.

With the gap closing Sandow ordered everyone to prepare for action. The *Warrior*'s crew were once again locked in their cabin. The Lewis gun was hauled up to the bridge and hidden inside of the wooden parapet. One of Duhig's Holy Grounders, wearing his old Royal Navy woollen jersey, stepped out on the foredeck. He carried a funnel shaped metal megaphone in one hand and the official admiralty envelope in the other. The king's harbour master's flag – a union jack with a white border and emblazoned in the centre with a Tudor crown, below which was inscribed the initials 'K.H.M.' – was run up the mast.

Sandow crouched out of sight on the bridge, while the rest of his team concealed themselves by lying in a line on the port deck right up against the gunwale. They cocked their revolvers and waited, feeling the resonating thud-thud of the hull as it rhythmically slapped the water.

The first mate of the *Upnor* was on watch when he spotted the *Warrior* to his stern on the port side and although familiar with the tugboat, he was surprised to see her rapidly approaching and flying the harbour master's flag. He called Capt. J. Hoar to join him on the bridge and from there they observed the tug's strange manoeuvring.

Once within earshot the deckhand on the *Warrior* waved the envelope shouting: 'message from the admiralty. Message from the admiralty'. The *Warrior* then sailed 400 metres past the *Upnor*, crossed its bow and dropped back on the starboard side. With both vessels parallel and pointing in the same direction, 100 metres apart, the sailor on the *Warrior* instructed them to send over a boat to collect their orders.

Since Hoar had no radio on board he was unable to verify whether the tugboat was actually bringing legitimate orders from Queenstown. Therefore, brushing aside any misgivings, he had the starboard lifeboat lowered and the second mate and four crew climbed in and rowed across. As they came alongside a sailor stood up with outstretched arm to accept the envelope; when Mick Murphy appeared out of nowhere, he lunged at the startled mariner and grabbing him by the scruff of the neck and the seat of his pants heaved him on board. Simultaneously the remainder of the crew found themselves staring into several pairs of revolvers. The five captives were quickly brought on deck and locked in the aft cabin along with the other prisoners. Con O'Sullivan stood guard over the hatchway.

Mick Murphy, Mick Burke, Peter O'Donovan, Seán

O'Donoghue and Tom Crofts jumped into the lifeboat and struggling against the current rowed as fast as they could. Capt. Hoar seeing the commotion ordered 'full steam ahead', but by then Sandow had mounted the Lewis gun on the parapet of the *Warrior*'s wheelhouse and was aiming it directly at the *Upnor*'s bridge. With his finger on the trigger he shouted at Hoar to cut his engines. Knowing that 'he was cornered' the captain was forced to comply, while Sandow kept an eye on the three-pounder gun in the bow of the *Upnor* – which could have easily sunk the *Warrior* – but to his relief it remained unmanned. Fortunately for him, it was a relic left over from the Great War.

As soon as the rowboat reached the *Upnor*, the five scrambled up the ladder at her side and onto the deck. Murphy with a Thompson gun at the ready, yelled: 'I'll shoot the shit out of any man that moves'. They rushed the bridge, confronting Hoar. 'We're taking this ship,' shouted Murphy, 'and if you resist I'll blow daylight through you.' The 'thunderstruck' captain attempted to stand his ground: 'This is piracy on the high seas and a hanging job' adding 'Mark you, questions will be asked about this in the House of Commons.'

But his protests were effortlessly brushed aside and according to Hoar: '[Murphy] ordered me to follow the *Warrior*. I refused and asked by whose authority. A pistol was placed at my head and I was told to have no argument and if I tried any trickery the lives of myself and the crew wouldn't be worth much, but if we went to our cabins and kept quiet we would not be harmed as they were not after the crew, only the cargo, and it was guaranteed that no personal effects or ship's stores would be touched.' Murphy made it clear to Hoar that if 'anything went wrong with the engines' he and his crew would be shot and with that any pretence of resistance crumbled. Hoar surrendered his revolver and the crew handed over two rifles.

Much to Sandow's relief Murphy signalled from the bridge that he was in control of the *Upnor*. Capt. Collins came alongside and John Duhig, together with his crew, jumped across, ready to take charge.

Despite his ordeal, Hoar appreciated the conduct and discipline of Murphy and his accomplices, who true to their word left the crew and their belongings alone. Even though Murphy was in a desperate rush to get going, he gave Hoar time to rehoist his lifeboat and agreed not to cut lose the barge filled with furniture that they were towing. For the rest of the voyage the crew were confined to their cabins.

Sandow convened the crew of the *Warrior* and according to the mate Charles Parker they were 'ordered to resume their watches and work our ship'. Sandow recalled the conversation differently and said that the crew told him 'they were quite willing' to resume their stations 'as they were tired of sitting about doing nothing'.

By now it was nightfall and to minimise the risk of being sighted by a Royal Navy patrol Sandow gave instructions for a blackout, with only the *Warrior*'s rear facing lamp acting as a beacon for the *Upnor* to follow. He then ordered Capt. Collins to turn around to the north and head straight for Ballycotton, fifty-five kilometres away – the same distance that they were from Roches Point.

The ships sailed in tandem into the darkness, with John Duhig at the wheel of the *Upnor*. Both crew – Duhig and his men on the *Upnor* and Parker and his fellow prisoners on the *Warrior* – rose to the occasion. No one on the *Warrior* tried to rush Sandow or Con O'Sullivan, nor did they attempt to sabotage the engine. It wouldn't have been too difficult for someone to release the boiler's safety vale thereby precipitously reducing the steam pressure, to turn the wheel valve to cut off the steam from powering the engine or to throw the engine into reverse by pulling the lever for the Stephenson valve.

Yet the stokers worked ceaselessly in the sweltering heat of the boiler room, Lewis Hills kept the engine well oiled and humming smoothly and Charles Regan took control of the ship's wheel and got into a friendly conversation with Capt. Collins. Collins told Regan that he was 'in the same predicament' and he went on to describe his kidnapping, likely with a view to protecting himself from any possible retribution.

Eventually at 11:30 they spotted Ballycotton lighthouse. Farther back the lights of the village formed a line along the edge of the cliff, which overlooked the broad shallow bay. At the foot of the cliff was their destination, the fishing pier. But the way was blocked by two rocky outcrops, Ballycotton Island – with the lighthouse – and the inner Small Island, and additionally by several treacherous reefs. Capt. Collins idled the engines and he and Sandow surveyed the scene, while the *Upnor* came up alongside on the starboard quarter.

The mariner was deeply pessimistic of their chances of

making it safely to the pier. Aside from the many rocks, which were either submerged or hidden by the darkness, the wind was beginning to pick up and there was a moderate swell. To compound matters there was virtually no light from the moon which was only a thin crescent.

Collins knew that these waters were notorious as the graveyard of countless ships and sailors. A government report in the mid nineteenth century warned: '[Ballycotton] is greatly exposed ... and not a little dangerous to mariners unacquainted with its coast.'

There was no safe passage between Small Island and the mainland – the shallow waters were traversed by a bed of rocks close to the surface. An alternative was the channel between the two islands known as Ballycotton Sound, which was around nine metres (5 fathoms) deep and almost 500 metres wide. However, it was obstructed by Sound Rock that was only visible at low tide. Therefore the *Warrior* would have had to sail east of the rock but still keep 150 metres away from the western side of Ballycotton Island which was skirted by rocks. What's more, the sound was subject to strong tidal currents. In the dead of night without any visibility, Collins dismissed this as a feasible option.

The only choice was to sail around and outside of the lighthouse and then make a sharp turn into the bay from the east. But even that was extremely perilous in the pitch dark. Without familiarity of the local conditions Capt. Collins realised that he couldn't bring both vessels safely in to anchorage – the obstacles were simply too numerous and too dangerous; he turned to Sandow and told him he couldn't land without a pilot to guide them in. Aside from the risk of drowning everybody, it would serve no purpose to have the *Upnor* go down with its precious cargo a few hundred metres from the shore

They had come so far, but it looked as if the whole elaborate scheme would come to naught. Sandow cursed Leahy, who should have been on board, and who was responsible for arranging for a pilot from Ballycotton to meet them; he was casting a long shadow on the operation. But certain that Seán O'Hegarty was in the vicinity, he ordered a sailor to use a lamp to send a Morse signal in the direction of the pier.

All this time, O'Hegarty had been waiting for news of the *Upnor*'s arrival. He had ordered the volunteers whom he sent to the pier to 'watch for the lights of two ships approaching' and he expected their signal by the early evening at the latest. But as hour after hour dragged on Seán became more worried. He was also cold and hungry, all of which made him even more foul tempered than usual.

In the virtually moonless night the scouts on the pier struggled to see anything at all. Then close to midnight the flashing light from the *Warrior* was sighted and they returned an acknowledgment in Morse. One of the volunteers unholstered a Very pistol and holding it with two outstretched arms he shot a flare high into the sky. A little later two men cautiously climbed into a rowboat and went out to meet the ships.

From the *Warrior* Sandow saw the rowboat approaching. Once within earshot the occupants hailed him and to his immense surprise it was Mick 'better late than never' Leahy with a local pilot by the name of Reardon. What Sandow said to Leahy has been lost to posterity, which may be for the better.

Reardon joined Mick Murphy and John Duhig on the bridge of the *Upnor* and as soon as it was high tide both ships raised steam again. With Jeremiah Collins carefully following, they made a wide turn around the lighthouse and then sailed in towards the pier. Just outside the harbour, the *Warrior* dropped anchor while the *Upnor* continued in.

Meanwhile back where the convoy was halted there was a shout and Seán looked up to see a bright light descend from the sky on a near vertical trajectory. It was time to move. Everybody hurried back to their lorries, Seán got into the lead motor car and they all headed towards the pier. They passed the small quaint Church of Ireland church with its weathered stone walls, slate roof and square tower and on their left was an immense black void concealing the bay. Above them, the sky was speckled with an infinite number of stars. The road steadily ascended from sea level into the village, which was strung out like a serpent on either side of the gently winding main street. On their left, the ground sloped down to the cliffs. They passed terraced houses, shops and pubs. To the right was the deserted RIC barracks which the brigade had once planned to attack until they found out that the police had been replaced by an army detachment.

Perched at the crest of the hill was the Bayview Hotel overlooking the lighthouse and the now invisible harbour. The road descended steeply for a few hundred metres, coming to a fork in the road. Seán had the trucks go to the right where they turned around and parked, while he drove a hundred metres further down onto the pier.

O'Hegarty stepped out of the car, pulled up the collar of his coat and stared intently at the approaching lights of the *Upnor* and the *Warrior*.

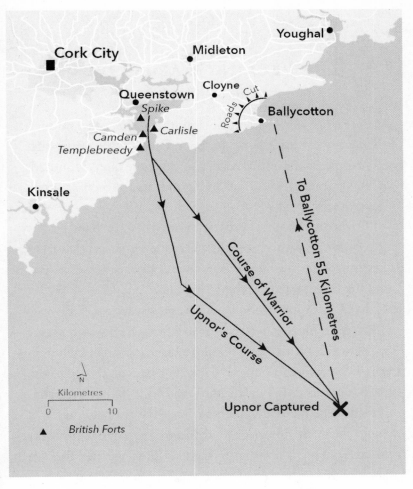

Youghal

Cork City

Midleton

Cloyne

Cut

Queenstown

Spike

Roads

Ballycotton

Carlisle

Camden

Templebreedy

Kinsale

Course of Warrior

To Ballycotton 55 Kilometres

Upnor's Course

N

Kilometres

0   10

▲ *British Forts*

Upnor Captured ✗

ROUTES OF THE *UPNOR* AND THE *WARRIOR*

15

THE FECKING WAR IS OVER

After the *Warrior* weighted anchor, the *Upnor* sailed through the narrow entrance of the harbour, between the breakwater and the pier and came to berth alongside the quay. Hundreds of IRA fighters and curious bystanders had gathered ashore. The crowd sent up a loud cheer.

On board there was a scurry of activity. Deckhands threw heavy hawsers onto the dock, where men grabbed them, ran them through the mooring rings and after a powerful pull tied the ropes, securing the *Upnor* fast.

Mick Murphy strode down the gangway; justifiably well satisfied. In his own words: '[Seán O'Hegarty] was standing on the pier … with a coat on him and he looked cold, but we were both cold and hungry. I thought he would be pleased, but he looked at me in his hard cold way. 'What kept you? he said. If he had said "fine man" or "that was a good job" I would have felt fine at once'. Murphy's arrogance probably ticked Seán off, but the chief was also likely worried that the delay in Queenstown had given the British sufficient time to learn what was going on and that they were already closing in, either by road or sea. He was doubtful whether he'd be able to unload the *Upnor* before they arrived.

Shortly afterwards Sandow came onshore in the *Warrior*'s dinghy and O'Hegarty put him in charge of the unloading. Sandow assembled a 'gang of locals' together with IRA volunteers and quickly went to work. They threw the furniture piled up on the deck overboard. Mick Leahy powered up the steam derrick, hoisted the launch lying on top of the hold and dropped it into the water. After the ropes securing the hold were cut, the heavy metal hatches were opened and Sandow jumped down.

Then he got the shock of his life. All he could see were cannon balls, hundreds and hundreds of cannon balls, nothing but fucking cannon balls. 'On top were cannon balls and they were so dry that we could walk across them. I was in despair I thought there was nothing but the cannon balls'. This time he thought to himself the British had bested him; he was beaten at his own game.

He and the others removed the cannon balls, dumping them overboard and in the process uncovering stacks of wooden crates. Someone handed Sandow a hammer and chisel and he opened the lid of one. To his delight there they were; carefully packed Lee Enfield rifles, well greased and in pristine condition. They had struck the mother lode. Mick Murphy exclaimed with delight: 'The fecking war is over'.

Sandow organised his workers with military precision. One group laboured in the hold, lifting the crates and using straps to attach them to the hook from the derrick. Once the crane swung the boxes up onto the quay, they were released by another group, who then passed them along to the three chains of men that extended back to the trucks at the edge of the pier.

Everyone worked as hard and as fast as they could, with only a matter of hours to undo what had taken at least two weeks to complete in Haulbowline. It was a tough, relentless, sweaty job. There were hundreds of cases of rifles, revolvers and machine guns and thousands of cases of ammunition, artillery shells and explosives. The workers in the bowels of the ship hurriedly opened crates to check whether they were worth taking and soon the floor was strewn with gunpowder, detonators, broken rockets and port-fires (hand held fuses). It was a miracle that no one carelessly lit a cigarette setting off a colossal explosion, the likes of which would be remembered to this day in Ballycotton.

On the pier they worked under the gleam of the arc lights that Seán had earlier directed to be strung up along the pier, supplemented by the *Upnor*'s lights and flares shot into the sky. O'Hegarty stood there recording the inventory in his notebook and barking orders as to where each fully laden lorry should be sent. The scene must have presented a surreal sight, resembling something out of a science fiction film or a H. G. Wells novel.

The lorries reversed down the hill onto the pier in groups of five for loading and were then driven off accompanied by an armed guard of four or five to their assigned destinations. The munitions were distributed all across the brigade area – some to Macroom, some to Knockraha – to be hidden in pre-prepared arms dumps and guarded round the clock by volunteers.

While the IRA was emptying the ship's hold, looters – several of them armed with revolvers and whom the navy later described as 'the peaceful inhabitants of Ballycotton' – swarmed onto the *Upnor* and its barge, where they stole everything and anything that wasn't bolted down. They took furniture, clothes, bedding and tools and made off with a barometer, binoculars, beds, blankets and books. They plundered mattresses, cutlery, tableware and even a pastry cutting board. Two armchairs, two galvanised iron baths, four dresses and four coats were carried off.

At 5:40 a.m. the sun rose behind Ballycotton Island, silhouetting the lighthouse, and spreading a beautiful orange red glow over the sky. The morning was crisp and bloody cold, just one or two degrees Celsius. Everyone was worn out and frozen to the bone; in Sandow's words they were 'drooping with exhaustion'. The Cork contingent, who had little to eat since the previous morning, were also famished. But they all continued working for another four hours. Admiral Gaunt later said that the locals were handed cheques for the considerable sum of £7.10s for their help, issued in the fictitious name of 'Rainey' of Queenstown. Although like much of Gaunt's intelligence, this is questionable.

But not everybody in Ballycotton was pleased. One self-described 'Loylast' dashed off a letter to Gen. Strickland:

Sir,

There is a German warship at Ballycotton with a cargo of war material of all sorts. There is about a 1,000 men unloading her and 100 of motors carrying it all over the country. It would be a good thing the Admiral attend to this. I am afraid Lloyd George took the troops away too soon.

Sir,

(Signed) A Loylast.

An infuriated lady – who was most likely the letter writer – phoned the telephone operator at the post office in a panic: 'The Germans are landing. Notify the authorities at once. They're swarming in!'

'That's dreadful madam. I'll do so at once', he assured her and then sat back and lit a cigarette. Throughout the night the IRA operator fielded numerous increasingly frantic calls from her: 'They are landing arms. There are two ships. Thousands of men'. And each time he patiently reassured her he was dealing with the matter.

Initially Sandow ordered the crew of the *Warrior* ashore, to spend the night under watch at the Bayview Hotel. However, he relented when they gave their word not to try to escape and raise the alarm. Able Seaman Charles Regan accompanied Sandow to the quay. There an IRA officer 'gave me £1 and told me to go to the hotel and get a bottle of whiskey and sent a man with me and he was told to force them to open the hotel. On our way up, there were crowds of men coming down from the village. They opened the hotel and I got the whiskey. I was ordered back to the quay again … and [told]… to take the whiskey on board and share it out, and [they] sent three men back with me, they relieved the guard that was left on board. After arriving on board, I went and turned in.' Lewis Hills reported: '[a guard] was stationed outside my berth all night long, with revolver in hand, and I was afraid to go to sleep'.

Mick Murphy returned to the *Upnor* and removed the ship's ensign from the flagpole, which he stuffed into his pocket as a souvenir. He then climbed down the ladder to the cabins to warmly greet Capt. Hoar: 'Come ashore and eat and drink as our prisoner'. To which Hoar replied: 'Certainly not sir – until I'm properly dressed.' A few minutes later, they headed over to the Bayview. Murphy was starving; claiming to have eaten only a single sausage all day.

Following a hearty meal they retired to the lounge for drinks, where they were likely joined by Capt. Collins, who relaxed in an armchair puffing on his pipe with a whiskey within easy reach. According to Murphy: 'Then we filled him [Capt. Hoar] with rum, brandy and whiskey and he said we were grand fellows'. Sitting there in comfort, they had a panoramic view of the orderly chaos on the pier below.

What quantity and what types of weapons and explosives did Seán O'Hegarty and Cork No. 1 capture?

To answer this question I have reviewed numerous secret documents, reports and telegrams. The sources are at times discrepant, partially because the British government, the admiralty and Ernest Gaunt all desperately wanted to downplay the size of the seizure. The principal estimates of the haul are those made by Gaunt, Admiral Browning in Devonport and other senior navy officers along with the audit compiled by the Royal Navy in July. This audit was part of the secret 'Admiralty Report on the Seizure of the *SS Upnor*' and included a 'list of armament stores deficient in the cargo'. However, this is incomplete and additional information can be gleaned from British and IRA communications and statements.

We can be certain that it was huge hoard as several hundred IRA volunteers and locals laboured for close to nine hours and managed to load seventy lorries. As Mick Burke succinctly put it: 'the quantity may be judged from the time taken to unload and the transport required to remove the cargo'. There were approximately 120 tons (120,000 kilograms) of munitions on board and both Sandow and Connie Neenan said that they 'emptied' the hold, as did Commander Candy, one of the first navy officers to inspect the looted *Upnor*.

Winston Churchill told the House of Commons that most of the weaponry on board was taken. Ernest Gaunt estimated that eighty tons (80,000 kilograms) of munitions were missing. Admiral Sir Montague Browning, the commander-in-chief at Devonport, who possessed the ship's bill of lading – a legal document containing an inventory of the cargo – corroborated these statements. On the other hand, Churchill, the admiralty and Gaunt claimed that the IRA missed a substantial portion of the small arms ammunition (SAA) on board.

Most authorities agreed that the IRA got away with thirty-three Lewis and six Maxim (or Vickers) machine guns. This at least doubled the total number of machine guns (aside from Thompson guns) already in the IRA's possession. The Lewis gun – nicknamed the 'Belgian rattlesnake' in the First World War – was an extremely effective weapon and a favourite of Cork No. 1, even though it had a tendency to jam and its ammunition drums only contained up to ninety-seven rounds, limiting its rate of fire. The Maxim was an even more formidable weapon, capable of firing 600 rounds per minute with a range of 2,000 metres (twice that of the Lewis gun). A 250 round belt fed it and the mechanism was so reliable that it was said the sole limiting factor on sustained fire was the ammunition supply.

Estimates of the number of rifles captured vary. Gen. Macready wrote at the time that it was 1,000, which is the same figure that Sandow remembered many years later. Mick Murphy said simply that 'there were cases upon cases of rifles'. The admiralty stated in July that only 449 rifles were taken.

O'Hegarty sent the munitions to various areas for safe-keeping, with the Donoughmore battalion, near Macroom, receiving 314 rifles. Since it's unlikely that he would have entrusted any one unit with more than a third of the cache, 1,000 seems like a conservative estimate.

The majority of these rifles were the Lee Enfield (SMLE); the regular army rifle of the Great War – accurate, dependable and deadly – it had a bolt action, an attached ten round magazine and a range of 500 metres.

The inventory of missing weapons compiled by the navy, in July 1922, included 697 Webley revolvers and fifty-one automatic revolvers, which seems to be reasonable numbers. The Webley was the standard British service revolver and was a mainstay of IRA urban fighting; it was 'robust, accurate and reliable'. The rotating cylinder held six large calibre .45 cartridges, which have been euphemistically stated as possessing 'excellent stopping power'. On the other hand, the Webley automatic, though highly accurate, had an overly complex firing mechanism making it capricious and unreliable.

O'Hegarty's greatest need by far was for ammunition. Until Ballycotton, his fighters had only a few rounds for each weapon, preventing him from mounting a viable campaign against either the Provisional Government or the British. Admiral Browning told the admiralty in early April that 'as far as is known' 1,440 cases of small arms ammunition (SAA), amounting to between 576,000 to 720,000 rounds, were missing. Similarly Macready wrote that 750,000 rounds were seized. Mick Murphy put the number at 500,000. However, as Gaunt stated the IRA likely overlooked a sizeable amount of the SAA and the navy's audit in July listed 169,498 rounds of .303 ammunition (suitable for both rifles and machine guns) as missing, along with 26,523 revolver .45 rounds and 2,557 Winchester .44 cartridges. Therefore it's clear that the brigade came away with at least 200,000 rounds.

Additionally the raiders captured 179,078 aiming tube rounds – low powered and with a short range – designed for training. Before that the IRA never had sufficient rounds to conduct target practice and so these cartridges, despite being of no use in combat, would enable them to improve the effectiveness of their riflemen. There were 25,352 blank cartridges, which had a propellant but no projectile (or bullet), that could be used to launch rifle grenades. It's entirely conceivable that the brigade converted at least some of these into live ammunition.

The hoard included a large quantity of explosives. Admiral Browning reported that 1,520 boxes of artillery shells, including four inch (102 mm) and twelve pounder (76 mm calibre) shells were missing. These weren't mentioned in the Royal Navy's investigation, though thousands of signal rocks and flares – all of which contained explosives – were. Having its own fully equipped munitions workshops Cork No. 1 was easily capable of removing the explosives from shells and rockets and constructing bombs and landmines. There were most likely cases of explosives and Maurice Brew of the Donoughmore IRA reported that his battalion hid forty-eight boxes of high explosives from the *Upnor*. Mick Murphy also confirmed that the brigade captured explosives.

There was a significant quantity of grenades and rifle grenades, which once again the navy failed to mention in its audit. A few days after the capture Gaunt sent a telegram to the admiralty stating there were no grenades left in the *Upnor*, which implied that the IRA did indeed capture a quantity of grenades, but thereafter the navy omitted any reference to them. Sandow estimated that they got '2,000 hand grenades and rifle grenades'. Independently Mick Burke said that they got 'grenades and rifle grenade throwers'.

Whereas the brigade was already well experienced in using grenades, rifle grenades were a new and highly effective weapon for them. The grenade launcher consisted of a metal cup attached to the front of the barrel of a Lee Enfield. The grenade (a modified Mills bomb) was inserted into the cup and by firing an aiming tube round or blank cartridge the shooter could propel the grenade 100-200 metres.

Lastly, there was an assortment of equipment including swords and bayonets (1,254), Very pistols (345), steel helmets (34), weapons' accessories and fuses and primers for bombs.

This was a game-changing haul. O'Hegarty could now dispense with his shotguns and obsolete rifles, and he'd be able to deploy heavily armed columns capable of large-scale, protracted attacks. If he had these a year earlier at Coolnacaheragh the Auxiliaries would never have escaped.

Eventually at 10 a.m. with the seventieth loaded lorry rumbling away Seán called a halt. It was already long past daylight and the British were sure to arrive soon and while everyone packed up and got ready to leave, the ten or so remaining lorries left empty.

An IRA officer – probably O'Hegarty – accompanied by four or five volunteers, rowed out to the *Warrior* and told the mate Charles Parker: 'they were taking away the guard and that we were to remain where we were for two hours and then we could proceed wherever we wished. If we left before two hours it was at our own risk'. Lewis Hills thought that the officer was the 'boss or ringleader' and he added that 'he was sorry he had put us to so much trouble, but from his point of view it was all necessary. The armed men that were on board then jumped into the boat and rowed ashore, leaving us to ourselves.'

Mick Murphy bid farewell to his drinking buddy, Capt. Hoar: 'I had taken his revolver when I went on board. It was a Webley .45 and when I shook hands with him before leaving, I said "goodbye captain, I hope you don't get into trouble over this". And I gave him back his Webley.'

It's a testament to the size of the haul that Murphy thought nothing of returning the revolver – something that would have been inconceivable only a day earlier.

Seán Hendrick, a city volunteer, hitched a lift on one of the lorries going to Macroom. To his frustration 'the lorry … crawled cautiously along, so he asked: "Can't you get any more out of this?"'

'I could,' said the driver, 'but it would be dangerous'. He jerked his thumb backwards at the cargo, 'We might all be blown to kingdom come'.

A weary Capt. Collins got into the back of a motor car, but after a short distance he discovered that he'd left his pipe in the hotel and insisted on returning to get it back. The IRA wary of the risk of him running into a British patrol sent Connie Neenan on Tim Hobbs' motorcycle to fetch them. So off the pair went, outwardly cheerfully obeying orders, but vigorously and colourfully cursing under their breath.

At 12.20 the *Warrior* hauled up anchor and headed towards Queenstown. By then, only the looters on board the *Upnor* remained busy. Mick Burke climbed into the back of the last lorry to leave when he saw 'a grey shape loomed up at sea' – the Royal Navy in the form of the destroyer *HMS Strenuous* had arrived on the scene.

16

HITTING THE FAN

Meanwhile at Admiralty House, Gaunt was frantic having read in his morning paper, the *Cork Constitution*, that the *Warrior* had apparently been hijacked. He sent an urgent telegram to the coastguard station at Land's End, on the south-western tip of England, asking whether they had sighted the *Upnor*, but the reply '*Upnor* not communicated [*sic*]' seemed to confirm his worst fears. Maybe the ship had broken down *en route* and the capture of the *Warrior* was merely a coincidence. But that was wishful thinking. It's said that when you're about to die your whole life flashes before you and for Ernest on that Thursday morning his whole career was flashing before him. It was never supposed to end this way.

By 10.30 he had ordered the destroyer *Strenuous* and the sloop *Heather* to 'raise steam for full speed' and find the *Upnor*. He telegraphed Admiral Browning in Devonport: '*Upnor* with small arms left Queenstown 1319 [hours] yesterday Wednesday for Devonport. It is reported that three hours [*sic*] later tug *Warrior* her master having being seized and ship filled with men proceeded full speed in same direction. I am sending *HMS Strenuous* in pursuit. Can you send a destroyer to meet …' Browning responded by dispatching two destroyers *HMS Veteran* and *Tormentor* to aid in the search. Gaunt then sent an encrypted telegram to the admiralty in London updating them on the situation.

As he sat there in his office in the basement of Admiralty House barking out orders and dictating telegrams, he likely kept his clerk Jack Kilty at his disposal. Unknown to him Kilty was an IRA agent.

The *Strenuous* powered out of the harbour, ahead of the *Heather*, and was soon making twenty-six knots, when at 1.30 p.m. she sighted the *Warrior* five and a half kilometres beyond Roches Point at Power Head. Capt. Louis Hamilton ordered an armed guard on board and after the crew told them what had happened, the two warships accompanied by the tugboat continued on to Ballycotton. By three o'clock the *Upnor* was found tied up at the pier; forlorn and pillaged.

Capt. Hamilton dispatched a boarding party to gather up the opened crates that were strewn all over the pier. The sailors, with marines keeping watch, readied the *Upnor* for the return to Queenstown and tied her half submerged motor-boat to the stern with a towing rope. Comd. Candy of the *Heather* reported: 'so far as is known no ammunition was recovered', his impression being that there were no munitions remaining on board.

Gaunt directed Candy to escort the *Warrior* to Devonport, but after the two ships had set sail he changed his mind and ordered them back to Queenstown. At 8 p.m. the *Warrior* moored in the outer anchorage of Cork Harbour, with an armed guard still on board and 'no communication whatever with the shore was to be permitted'. Finally Len Williams came on board, having been released from the Rob Roy Hotel earlier that afternoon

A few hundred metres away at Haulbowline the *Upnor*

was moored alongside the quays, where dockers set about the dangerous task of clearing the ransacked hold and officers determined what was missing and what remained.

Gaunt was going to conduct a thorough investigation and hopefully in the process find a scapegoat. Navy officers took written statements from the crews of the *Warrior* and the *Upnor* and the admiral himself questioned Leonard Williams and Andrew Horne.

But the first thing Ernest did was to contact Mick Burke, in the mistaken belief that he was now responsible for maintaining law and order on behalf of the Provisional Government. According to Burke: 'Returning to Cobh, I went to bed and a few hours afterwards was called and told the admiral wanted to speak to the OC Cobh IRA. I spoke on the phone to him. He said he would like to see me. With Volunteer Denis Duggan, I called on the admiral, who told me what had happened to the *Upnor*. I said I knew nothing about it and added I would take up the matter immediately with headquarters. He seemed pleased with the interview, so much for British intelligence'. Gaunt however sent a terse telegram to the admiralty: 'Have seen head of local Free State police, quite useless'.

Gaunt placed the *Warrior* 'under arrest' and he treated Williams as if he was guilty of piracy; forcing him to surrender his service revolver. In an aggressive interrogation he asked the captain: 'You know that your ship has been seized and has been committing [*sic*] piracy on the high seas?' 'I was taken out of her', Williams replied, matter of factually. Further questioning yielded no useful information and uncovered no evidence to indicate that the captain had cooperated in any way with the IRA. But Ernest resolved not to leave any stone unturned so when Williams subsequently returned to England, he sent a telegram: 'suggest detectives ascertain if master of *Warrior* possesses unusual amount of money'.

Assisting Gaunt in his inquiry was his district intelligence officer Capt. Crick of the Royal Marines whose knowledge of the situation in Cork was on par with that of the admiral. Apparently acting on information from 'a secret informer' Crick decided that 'the Free Staters were also implicated' and they had sent an officer down from Dublin by the name of Cronin 'to organise the raid'. Unwilling to give the IRA any credit he surmised: 'the looted arms do not appear to have been collected in central depots, at least to any extent systematically. The raiders and those who unloaded the ship appear to have taken as many as they could carry for their own use and for distribution to their friends'.

Crick seemed to get a lead when two British lieutenants reported that 'in the billiard room of the Royal Cork Yacht Club last night, 2nd April … [a merchant marine officer Frederick Collins] openly boasted to us that he knew all about the *Upnor* case on the night previous to her capture. He stated that he was in the presence of a number of men on Tuesday night, 29th March [*sic*, should be the 28th], who were discussing how they were going to commandeer the tug *Warrior* and capture the *Upnor*. On being asked why he did not report this to the naval authorities, he replied he was not going "to run the risk of being shot in the back" '. Then in a strange coincidence three nights after the encounter in the yacht club Collins' ship the *SS Vellavia* was raided by the Cobh IRA and two rifles along with 100 rounds were captured.

Crick deducted that if the IRA planned all along to seize the *Warrior* then Len Williams must have deliberately returned to Queenstown with the *Medusa* in tow and that he was therefore a party to the conspiracy. However, Collins' statement was merely a drunken boast; since Sandow decided to capture the *Warrior* at the last minute after the intended target, the *Hellespont*, unexpectedly put to sea and no other suitable ship was available. Gaunt passed his information on to London for further inquiry, though nothing came of it but a statement that 'Mr Collins is suspected of having assisted in the raid [on the *Vellavia*] and is reported to be openly in sympathy with the Republicans'.

On the other hand, Gaunt managed to identify Jeremiah Collins as the person 'who acted as captain of the *Warrior*', but what use was that when Collins had been kidnapped in public and therefore couldn't be implicated? He also concluded that Tom Barry was the 'leader of the gang', though when he had a photo of Barry 'as a boy of 17' shown to Capt. Hoar and his mate they drew a blank. Despite this, Strickland's intelligence officer reported: 'T. B. (Bernie) Barry is now the leading man in Cork ... His prestige will have been greatly enhanced by his recent successful exploit, i.e. the capture of the *Upnor*'. His comrades called Barry many things, but 'Bernie' was not one of them.

At the same time Macready's intelligence assessment

commenting on the 'daring outrage' remarked that: 'As far as can be at present ascertained, T. B. Barry a dangerous Republican extremist was in command of the operation on land'.

Gaunt complained to Andrew Horne: 'I am unable to understand why you did not inform me immediately when *Warrior* was commandeered on Wednesday afternoon'. And he wrote to his superiors: 'I regret that the agents of the 'Warrior' did not inform me of her being commandeered, but all civilians live in such fear of their lives that they will take no action against the forces of disorder'.

Horne wasn't prepared to be the fall guy. Furious that Gaunt's efforts were likely to damage his 'reputation and position as a law abiding subject' he sent a letter to the admiralty, in which – even though Sandow had pulled a gun on him – he disingenuously claimed that he thought that he was dealing with legitimate representatives of the Provisional Government. 'It was emphatically stated that the tug was required by that government. I of course had no idea that there was anything wrong ... [and that I was instead dealing with] the extremists'.

But it was his conclusion that was damming: 'I was quite unaware of the departure of the *Upnor* or of anything in connection with her and I am sure the fact of the vessel having left this port unarmed, unescorted and without wireless ... clearly indicates no one had any idea that she would be interfered with by anybody'. As Horne was alluding to it was ultimately Gaunt who was at fault and no amount of obfuscation and blaming could hide his responsibility.

In contrast, Capt. Hoar was one of the few central figures fully exonerated and the admiralty wrote: 'No blame seems to attach to the master of the *Upnor*. He might have made more show of resistance, but his only effective course would seem to have been to take steps to sink the ship before the Republicans came on board and he could hardly have been expected to realise the position in time to take such drastic action'.

Ultimately Gaunt's investigation yielded nothing but a net full of red herrings; no one whom he named, suspected or accused had any role in planning or leading the attack. The only potential lead was Crick's reference to a number of local sailors who may or may not have been members of the IRA's crew on the *Warrior*: George Gazley an ex-Irish Guards sergeant, Botteley the son of an RIC constable and Corcoran who worked at Haulbowline. There was no mention of Seán O'Hegarty, who remained a largely unknown and mysterious figure. It was ironic that the sole member of the IRA whom Gaunt unwittingly turned to for help was Mick Burke who played a pivotal role in the operation.

Over the course of the next few days, Gaunt gave varying estimates of the quantity of munitions seized. On Thursday, the day he retrieved the *Upnor*, he stated: 'All arms and ammunition removed from *Upnor*. A few stores left'. The following day he reassured the admiralty that the 'raiders were disturbed by news of [the] destroyers raising steam and only got away [with] eighty tons'. His use of the adverb 'only' being entirely self-justifying.

The next week he added that thirty-two tons (32,000

kilograms) of SAA remained on board; this comprised all the ammunition originating from the stores on Rocky Island, whereas the ammunition being returned by the marines and coastguard was taken.

Even if O'Hegarty and his brigade had overlooked a large quantity of SAA hidden deep in the hold, they had undoubtedly discovered a considerable amount. Furthermore Gaunt's figure of a total haul of eighty tons of missing munitions, correlates with most other sources, both British and Irish. Even for a regular army, this was a lot, but for the IRA it was unprecedented. The organisation had never before seized or handled such a huge amount of war *matériel*.

To add to Gaunt's humiliation, the newspapers had a field day. The *Cork Examiner* reported under a headline 'Cork Harbour Sensation' that 'official reticence is being maintained with regard to the whole affair, but it is admitted, even in naval circles that it was a well thought out clever move [to capture the *Warrior* first in order to seize the *Upnor*]' adding that 'naval men here ... all admit [that the navy was] cleverly outwitted'. The *Constitution* calling it 'The Week's Sensation' wrote that 'It was a daring coup, cleverly conceived and brilliantly carried out. There were we understand no casualties'.

The *Irish Independent* wrote that it was 'a clever and daring coup' and 'an amazing exploit', noting that 'there was no armed guard over the cargo of arms and ammunition'. In an article titled 'Piracy on Cork Coast' the pro-unionist *Irish Times* called it a 'remarkable exploit'. Most significantly, the London *Times* referred to it as 'a clever and daring coup'. The *Daily Express* ran a headline 'De Valera's New Fleet?

Mystery of a Runaway Tug'. Across the Atlantic, the *New York Times* remarked that it was a 'sensational affair … carried out with great audacity'.

These papers – all of which opposed the anti-Treaty IRA – were incredulous at the complexity and ingenuity of the operation and alluded to the incompetence of the Royal Navy. Although Gaunt was not mentioned by name, it was obvious to those in authority that he was responsible for the debacle and for sullying the navy's reputation. To be criticised in the media was unpleasant, but to be ridiculed was a far more dreadful fate.

Presumably members of the London clubs and senior naval officers received the news with a mixture of incredulity and laughter. 'Poor Gaunt, I'm afraid the old boy has lost it' and 'Dreadful state of affairs'. Even Gaunt was forced to admit 'the coup was cleverly planned and carried out' and was only able to muster an anaemic defence on his own behalf: 'it did not occur to anyone, as far as I am aware, that any overt actions upon the high seas might be anticipated'.

In London, the British government reacted with horror. Gen. Strickland recorded in his diary: 'cabinet etc. very upset over "Upnor" being taken and arms lost'. Gen. Macready gave a more vivid description: 'I cannot remember having seen such a gale blowing as was raging in Downing Street and the War Office'. Going on to compare the atmosphere to that at the outbreak of the First World War: 'Even … the Declaration of War in '14 was as nothing to the wild excitement consequent on the capture by Mr. Barry of one of His Majesty's ships of war'.

But Macready had by then washed his hands of the whole Irish business, blaming the failure of British policy on the government and particularly Winston Churchill and he reacted with amusement to the government's dilemma: 'It really was too funny, but very wearing'.

On Friday evening, the day after the recovery of the *Upnor*, Macready attended an emergency meeting at the Colonial Office convened by Churchill, where 'It was agreed that the incident should be given no more public attention that was necessary'. All of Churchill's future statements minimising the haul – which contradict evidence from multiple other reliable sources – should be interpreted in the light of this assertion.

The meeting additionally concluded 'that any breach of naval discipline which might be found to have occurred should be severely punished'. And in future 'it was decided that ships carrying warlike stores [from Ireland] should proceed under naval escort'.

Andy Cope, the assistant under-secretary for Ireland, reported from Dublin that: 'This is a bad blow for P. G. [the Provisional Government] and it will result in the going over to the other side of the whole IRA in the Cork area … It has given considerable confidence to the insurgent IRA throughout the country … I must tell you the situation is very rocky'. Cope didn't attribute the seizure solely to a combination of IRA ingenuity and navy incompetence and surmised: 'There must have been collusion in getting the *Upnor* into Ballycotton.

Churchill wrote in a report he prepared for the cabinet: 'There is no doubt that the Irish have a genius for conspiracy rather than for government. The government is feeble, apologetic, expostulatory: the conspirators active, audacious and utterly shameless ... The Queenstown episode clearly shows that we are in contact with revolutionaries who will stop at nothing, who are capable of brilliantly conceived operations and who have facilities and resources at their unhampered disposal both in money and arms and of a kind and on a scale never previously experienced'.

Due to the extensive press coverage, Churchill had to make a statement to the House of Commons. Though first he had to decide on how much munitions he would admit were taken. If the figure was too low he would appear disingenuous, whereas if he was to be forthright this would only add to the Royal Navy's and the government's humiliation.

Estimates already issued by Ernest and Admiral Browning in Devonport were far too high to release. The former of which consisted of eighty tons of munitions and the latter of which included up to 720,000 rounds of small arms ammunition (SAA). However, on 3 April Admiral Sir Roger Keyes presented Churchill with much more palatable numbers: 'The Deputy Chief of the naval staff stated that the quantity of arms captured from the store ship 'Upnor' did not exceed 381 rifles, 727 revolvers, 978 sword bayonets'. Two days later the admiralty wrote to Churchill's office stating that 'information has now been received from Queenstown [in other words Gaunt] that the greater part of the small arms and ammunition in *Upnor* was not taken by the rebels' and having largely agreed with Admiral Keyes on the quantity of weapons added that 25,000 rounds of SAA were also missing.

Both of these last two reports made no mention of explosives.

In Gaunt's later telegrams to the Admiralty on 3 and 4 April – filed in the 'Admiralty Report on the Seizure of the *SS Upnor'* – he avoided repeating his assessment of eighty tons and instead evasively emphasised what SAA remained in the *Upnor* rather than what was actually taken. Though he added that 'no cases of rifles or pistols, no machineguns or grenades remain'. Notably he made no mention of only 25,000 rounds of SAA being captured and he never said that most of the munitions weren't taken.

It's intriguing to wonder why the navy sent Churchill figures that differed so much from what admirals Gaunt and Browning reported. Did Churchill's office put pressure on the admiralty to do so? Did the admiralty either deliberately or inadvertently misinterpret Gaunt's telegrams? The estimates given by Admiral Keyes were so minimal that they failed to explain how the *Upnor* could have left Queenstown fully laden, nor why Seán O'Hegarty needed seventy lorries to cart away the loot. The figures were also considerably less than those from the navy's final audit in July, which listed almost 200,000 rounds of SAA.

When Churchill eventually spoke to the House of Commons he decided to present these lower estimates, with some modifications. On 3 April he listed the number of weapons given by Keyes, plus 500,000 rounds of SAA and 'a small quantity of explosives' and two days later he clarified that the SAA 'cannot exceed 25,000 rounds'. Though he did state incongruously that 'the greater part of the arms and ammunition on board were unloaded' at Ballycotton.

However, he was forced to take responsibility: 'I am bound to admit that an inalienable responsibility rests with the British government to safeguard in all circumstances arms and munitions of war which are in their hands'. Although he blamed the Provisional Government for failing to maintain control in Cork, he conceded: 'As a matter of fact, the Provisional Government have I think certain grounds of complaint against us for having allowed, no doubt under very difficult circumstances, these things to pass out of the hands of the British government into the hands of those who are at least as much the enemies of the Provisional Government as they are of the British government.'

A Liberal Party MP, Lieut-Col John Ward asked Churchill: 'Is the right honourable gentleman aware that this conspiracy was discussed in certain clubs in London last week and how is it that officials of the government, or their intelligence department, were not in a position to acquaint themselves with what was going to happen?' Which of course was unsubstantiated rubbish.

The Conservative member Sir William 'Jix' Joyson-Hicks wanted to know: 'What action is the government taking to recover their own property and to bring those pirates to justice? Churchill was evasive, reluctant to admit that the answer was 'nothing'. Though he subsequently clarified: 'We certainly are not going to take measures in the interior of Ireland to recover these goods'.

The parliamentary secretary to the admiralty, Leo Amery, was likely the only member to praise Gaunt in the House: 'I desire to add, however, that the prompt action of the Commander-in-Chief of the Western Approaches in sending a destroyer and a sloop in pursuit, immediately he knew of the suspicious circumstances attending the sailing of the tug *Warrior*, prevented the greater part of the cargo being removed from the *Upnor*'.

The estimates Churchill gave to the House were inaccurate and misleading, especially regarding the quantity of SAA and explosives and in all probability this was deliberate. Churchill, who had a reputation for being knowledgeable and having a hands-on approach when it came to naval matters, was unlikely to have believed them himself. After all, he had committed himself to downplaying the incident. For instance, how could the quantity of SAA missing suddenly have been reduced to 25,000 rounds? How did he decide that only 'a small quantity' of explosives was looted and at the same time admit that most of the cargo had been taken? Churchill was either a fool or a liar.

Nevertheless his speeches had their desired effect and thereafter the *Upnor* incident faded from public discussion. Next he had to deal with Michael Collins.

The Provisional Government was apoplectic. When Macready met Collins a few days afterwards he 'found him in a very anxious frame of mind'. On 3 April, the same day he spoke to the Commons, Churchill further aggravated the situation by sending Collins the text of his speech including the paragraph where he called the seizure 'a gross and dishonourable breach of the Truce' that was due in part to the Provisional Government's 'practically non-existent' presence in Cork.

Michael Collins, refusing to accept that the capture was due to the navy's ineptitude, replied: 'It is generally believed here that there was collusion between those responsible on your side and the raiders. Also generally believed that the capture was enormously larger than is stated in your wire … Provisional Government strongly feel that the safety of these arms entirely a question for your Admiralty'.

Collins said the incident showed 'how desirous certain sections of the English military authorities were to arm Irish men against each other'. An opinion that was echoed by Liam de Róiste: 'It is pretty evident that there was deliberate 'negligence' in the guarding of the vessel'.

Macready wrote to Field Marshal Henry Wilson: 'Poor Michael is distressed that we hand over arms to Mr Barry of Cork from men o'war and we won't give him any.'

Churchill tried to assuage Collins. He assured him that 'there was no collusion', that his figures for the capture 'covers all important items' and that he'd forward to him as soon as possible a 'full list of losses'. He clarified that the Royal Navy was responsible for the safety of the cargo and that 'the most stringent precautions will be taken in future for safeguarding all arms whether by land or sea'. He also authorised 'Mr Cope to issue rifles up to 6,000 in all and 4,000 revolvers at once' for Collins' National Army and police force. Less than two weeks later he increased this by another 2,000 rifles and twenty Lewis guns.

Somewhat surprisingly – and foolishly – the admiralty later submitted a malicious damages claim to the Free State seeking £29,720 in compensation for loss of armament stores and £252 for looted private property. An astute civil servant in the British treasury warned, that 'unless there be something to lead to the inference that these things were taken for the purpose of damaging or destroying them I am of opinion that a claim on the basis of malicious damage ought not succeed … I do not see why the robbers could not have used the things they took in this case.' Another treasury official agreed that the episode involved 'looting' and not 'malicious damage', adding: 'the fact that there was what would be legally negligence in letting the "rebels" get this ammunition'.

In response the Free State's Director of Intelligence, Col Michael Costello, prepared a report, stating: 'It is alleged that the captain of the 'Upnor' [Capt. Hoar] connived at the affair and it is believed that he received a good sum. His ship was constantly in Haulbowline and he was always in company with IRA leaders'. This allegation appeared to be completely without foundation.

However, the conclusion of Costello's document was more significant: 'I am of opinion that the British authorities were guilty of gross negligence in as much that if they did not arrange to hand over the arms to the Irregulars [anti-Treaty IRA] they certainly did not take the required precautions to prevent a seizure. It will be agreed that a ship loaded with such a valuable cargo of war material should have been properly escorted by a warship and also carrying a complement of soldiers or sailors. It has not been possible to obtain definite evidence to support the assertion that the arms were deliberately handed over to the Irregulars, but from the facts above stated and the circumstances existing in the country at the time, it would appear that such was the case.'

Eventually the Free State government wrote to the British government refusing to pay up and adding 'we consider that we have a very serious grievance against your naval authorities on this score'.

While all of this was going on, one has to ask what was Admiral Gaunt's fate?

It can be argued that throughout his long career Gaunt made only two major errors. The first was in 1920 when he publicly criticised Admiral Sir David Beatty's actions during the Battle of Jutland, which was foolish given that Beatty was both the First Sea Lord and a close ally of Churchill's. The second was the capture of the *Upnor*. These mistakes were about to compound each other.

On 3 April when Churchill called a second meeting to discuss the incident, Beatty, in his capacity as the professional head of the navy, was in attendance and according to the minutes there was a discussion about disciping Gaunt: 'It was urged that if exception was to be taken to the conduct of the naval commander-in-chief, Queenstown this officer should, in fairness to himself, be tried before a Court Martial.'

The admiralty demanded that Gaunt provide a 'full written report... on the circumstances, having special regard to the reason why no guard was placed on board and no arrangement was made for the escort of this vessel'. They also sent him an unusually curt telegram, with Beatty's name on the distribution list: 'Cannot understand delay in providing information [regarding the quantity and description of the seized munitions] ... You have had four days to obtain the information we require'.

Macready reported: 'I believe they want to try the admiral by Court Martial and God knows what else' and in his own inimitable turn of phrase compared Gaunt's situation to that of the unfortunate John the Baptist: 'people in London [were] metaphorically demanding the head of the Admiral in a charger [plate]'. While Churchill in his presentation to the cabinet referred to the incident as 'the regrettable loss – to use no stronger term – by the Admiralty of important munitions which were in their charge'.

If Ernest were court martialled his whole world would come crashing down. At a stroke, his carefully constructed career and reputation would be ruined. His sense of self-worth, dependent on a lifetime of service to the king and empire, would be demolished. He and Louise would become social outcasts.

There were however two things in Ernest's favour. The first was his amiable relationship with George V who likely would have put in a good word for his beleaguered admiral. But the second, much more important, factor was that Ernest had screwed up monumentally and it's sometimes better to make a massive blunder, rather than commit a minor gaffe. If the admiralty held a court martial it would bring unwanted attention to its own culpability; it was definitely in the navy's and government's interest to let the matter die down.

Anyhow Gaunt's stint in Queenstown was coming to a

natural end and in May he returned to London; in his stead Mick Burke moved into Admiralty House and raised the republican Tricolour. With the writing on the wall, the navy placed Gaunt on half-pay and left him without a command.

In 1923 the king invested him as a Knight Commander of the British Empire (KCB) in what should have been a cause for great celebration, though at the same ceremony his predecessor Admiral Tupper received the more prestigious Knight Grand Cross of the British Empire (GBE). According to his daughter Sheila: '[father] was absolutely furious [with his KCB] and told me he was going to return it, but Ireland was his graveyard or rather the graveyard of his career. The Order of the British Empire had a very bad reputation, because during the First World War it had been doled out to all and sundry and therefore sank in value.'

Shortly afterwards, in a symbolic gesture, he was appointed a full admiral, which goes to show that in the navy failure can be a pathway to promotion. In 1925, after forty-seven years of service, Ernest retired. Seemingly oblivious to how lucky he was to escape with his reputation largely intact, albeit contused.

Nevertheless he lost any possibility of being appointed a governor in Australia and Downing Street wrote to the admiralty: 'It may be of value to you to know privately that Admiral Gaunt is not likely to be offered the State Governorship in Australia for which he is a candidate'.

17

CIVIL WAR

In Cork Seán O'Hegarty was in an unassailable position. Even Winston Churchill admitted: 'this undoubtedly makes the mutinous section of the Cork IRA by far the most heavily armed party in that district.' But instead of going on the attack O'Hegarty opted for a defensive strategy: 'We'll hold Cork ... We'll leave nobody into Cork, but we won't fight'. His attitude however merely delayed – rather than averted – the onset of civil war, given that Michael Collins and the Provisional Government couldn't possibly allow the Cork IRA to determine the extent of its jurisdiction.

But suddenly Seán changed his position and it's difficult to know why this happened. Perhaps when he attended the convention in Dublin he saw how divided the IRA were amongst themselves and how they lacked any coherent plan of action. Maybe when Collins visited Cork in March Seán realised the extent of popular support for the Treaty. Maybe his brother Patrick Sarsfield who was close to Collins persuaded him to acknowledge the Treaty as the will of the people. Perhaps the impending catastrophe of an internecine war forced the intensely logical O'Hegarty to reevaluate his stance. Or maybe it was a combination of all these and other factors.

Seán didn't personally 'accept' the Treaty and he never moderated in his contempt for the agreement and the Free

State. But he fully understood the tragedy of a civil war tearing the country apart and the unlikelihood – at least for now – of securing a Republic. He pleaded with his comrades: 'All that is needed now is for someone irresponsible to pull a trigger and we will have a civil war with all its horrors right in our land.'

His new role as a peacemaker caught many by surprise; until then he had never been one to compromise. Liam de Róiste wrote: 'Seán Hegarty [*sic*] does not want trouble in Cork city and is desirous of coming to some arrangement to avoid it. He had a conversation with Collins the other day and Micheál told me he found Seán the most reasonable man "on the other side".' O'Hegarty had rarely, if ever, been called 'reasonable', though De Róiste qualified his statement: 'He desires of course to be the chief in Cork'.

In May Seán was even invited to address the Dáil – several of whose members he had previously threatened with assassination – and in a speech laden with uncharacteristic eloquence and poignancy he stated: 'I have seen it in speeches quite plainly expressed – that the Republic cannot be maintained unless there is civil war. What does civil war mean? To my mind ... that you break the country so utterly and leave it in such a way that England simply walks in and has her way as she never had it before ... You [will] break the country utterly and destroy any idea of a Republic'.

Remarkably O'Hegarty's reasoning had become similar to that of Collins'. While Collins called the Treaty a 'stepping stone' to a Republic, O'Hegarty argued 'when the opportunity comes to set up a Republic it can be set up.'

O'Hegarty acted as an intermediary between Collins and Mulcahy and the anti-Treaty side. It has even been suggested that by this stage he and Mulcahy were 'enjoying a good relationship'. Although Seán's efforts came extremely close to averting conflict, he ultimately failed. Finally in June with his brigade officers refusing to compromise and armed conflict over control of the Four Courts in Dublin imminent Seán resigned as commandant of Cork No. 1. But true to form his last warning to his comrades was that if they decided to fight then there should be no holding back. Mick Leahy succeeded him and Sandow was appointed vice-commander.

On 28 June civil war erupted when the National Army attacked the Republican garrison in the Four Courts – with the help of artillery loaned to them by Gen. Macready. In August the National Army took Cork city, forcing the Republicans to retreat into the countryside and in May 1923 the IRA conceded defeat and laid down their arms. Without O'Hegarty and without a clear strategy the Cork fighters were disorganised, demoralised and disparate. Tom Crofts said: 'the absence of Seán O'Hegarty in the Civil War had a very bad effect'.

It was a short bloody conflict, with almost as many casualties as the War of Independence, but more vicious and with a bitter legacy, which lasted for over fifty years. One of its greatest tragedies occurred in August when Michael Collins travelled to Cork and met with Seán O'Hegarty in a final attempt to arrange a ceasefire. The following day, the 22nd, he was ambushed and killed at Beál na Bláth in west Cork. Tom Hales – the brother of Donal Hales in Genoa – was in charge of the ambush. Whether the Lee-Enfields used in the ambush or the bullet that killed him came from the *Upnor*, we'll never know, but it's highly likely.

Mick Leahy remembered being in Ballyvourney along with Mick Murphy and Éamon de Valera when they learned that Collins had died: 'Mick Murphy burst out laughing, but Dev turned around and said "it's nothing to laugh at when an Irishman is killed by another".'

Thereafter, with the cold, methodical Mulcahy in charge, the National Army waged a remorseless, unyielding war. Mulcahy was responsible for the execution of more prisoners than the British in the course of the War of Independence and Tom Crofts called him 'bitter and vindictive'.

The *Upnor* stockpile enabled the Cork IRA to mount a robust challenge to Collins and the National Army especially in the opening months of the conflict. Its cache accounted for most of the ammunition, rifles and machine guns and a substantial portion of the explosives in its possession. Furthermore it was all military grade ordnance, as distinct from the often improvised, antiquated and homemade weaponry that they were hitherto accustomed to using.

At the time of the Truce in July 1921, it has been estimated that the IRA's 1st Southern Division – comprising the Cork, Kerry, Waterford and west Limerick brigades – possessed only 50,000 rounds of ammunition. Therefore, the capture of 200,000 or more rounds was crucial for the anti-Treatyites.

Patrick Maume, wrote: 'This single exploit supplied much of the arsenal used by the republican forces in Munster during the civil war'. Florence O'Donoghue commented that between the Truce and the Civil War, 'the only substantial acquisitions of arms which the anti-Treaty forces received' were from the *Upnor*, a raid on Clonmel RIC barracks and a shipment landed at Waterford. With the *Upnor* being by far the largest of these.

Gen. Macready noted that: 'this seizure turns the balance heavily against the Provisional Government'. A leading Free State official complained: 'If the British forces had not negligently permitted the capture of this vessel by Republicans, the latter forces would have been much more easily suppressed since a large part of their arms were derived from the stores on board the *Upnor*'. A senior British civil servant admitted: 'By this mischance the rebels got vast stores of ammunition and prolonged their resistance'.

The Cork fighters adjusted their tactics in response to the unaccustomed availability of weapons and ammunition. In the early summer of 1922 Cork 1 attempted to model itself after a regular army, deploying large columns and instead of ambushing relied on prolonged firefights supported by heavy machine gun fire. Nevertheless the better armed and better led National Army relentlessly pushed them back. Dan Breen of Tipperary remarked: 'The Republican columns, which had been trained to [*sic*] guerrilla warfare, were utterly unable to adapt themselves to [more conventional] line fighting. Moreover at this opening stage of the war they had no heart for the fight. They did not want this war of brother against brother.'

Multiple accounts reference the *Upnor* haul. Patrick

McHugh, an IRA munitions officer reported: 'The Cork men were well armed as they had captured the *Upnor* and had large quantities of rifles and ammunition, also machine guns'. In July, Maurice Brew of Donoughmore near Macroom reported that his battalion stored munitions from the *Upnor*, including 300 Lee-Enfields, fourteen machine guns, 86,000 rounds of ammunition and forty-eight boxes of high explosives. Capt. Somerville of the Royal Navy had information about a hundred strong IRA unit operating at Mitchelstown, north Cork; 'many have new' Lee Enfield rifles and 'all had revolvers'. Mick Murphy said that rifles from the *Upnor* were supplied to the IRA in Kerry, which was the scene of some of the heaviest and most brutal fighting in the Civil War.

The brigade's acquisition of large quantities of explosives and detonators had dire consequences and over the course of the Civil War much of Cork's infrastructure was destroyed. The IRA attempted to prevent the National Army from encroaching by severing communications with the rest of the country. They blew up roads, railways and bridges and burned numerous public buildings, leading to long lasting economic devastation and hardship.

In January 1923, the Great Southern and Western Railway Company reported that in the previous twelve months its lines had been damaged in 375 places, 42 engines had been derailed and fifty-one bridges destroyed. For most of the war there was no direct rail link between Dublin and Cork, prompting one Free State politician to comment: 'There never has been a case of any country in which such a fierce attack was made on its railway system.'

Queenstown and its surroundings suffered like every-where else and when the National Army landed in early August, Mick Burke and his fighters set fire to Admiralty House, Belmont Hutments and the Military Hospital before escaping.

Nearby Belvelly bridge was demolished, which Burke had failed to blow up the previous year when he had just a few kilograms of gelignite. In addition part of the harbour at Ballycotton was blown up with the intention of thwarting an expected landing by the National Army.

Without Seán O'Hegarty and Cork No. 1's taking of the *Upnor* the Civil War would have been shorter and less intensely fought, with lower casualties and less destruction. The sudden increase in munitions just before the outbreak of hostilities likely dissuaded leaders from seeking a compromise and encouraged volunteers to join the fight.

So ends the story of the most astonishing military operation carried out in Ireland in the last hundred years. It was almost flawless in its planning and execution. Seán O'Hegarty, Sandow and his squad were cool, efficient and professional, as well as extremely lucky. Above all the operation was a testament to O'Hegarty's leadership and his ability to select and train such a capable force.

Florence O'Donoghue wrote: 'In organisation and in execution, in the secrecy with which the plans were kept and in the measures taken for security and distribution this was a brilliant operation, carried out and under the orders and direction of the Brigade Commandant Seán O'Hegarty'.

However, the greatest accolades were those accorded by his enemies including Ernest Gaunt, Gen. Macready and most notably by Winston Churchill who described it as a 'brilliant' operation.

Mick Murphy was delighted that the capture was significant enough to be debated in the House of Commons, commenting: 'That *Upnor* skipper was right. It was raised in the House of Commons, sure enough. I hope the poor man did not get into trouble'

It is interesting – and salutary to note – that none of the admirals, generals, intelligence officers, politicians and journalists who investigated or commented on the seizure of the *Upnor* ever fully understood the operation or whom the protagonists were. They were blinkered by their biases, preconceptions and ignorance and frequently by their incompetence.

Remarkably during the operation, no one was killed, wounded or shot at. The strongest complaint I came across was that of John Gear, the cook on the *Warrior*, who was over-worked cooking non-stop for the hijackers. Andrew Horne was released unharmed based on his word of honour, Capt. Hoar was given a few drinks too many and had his revolver returned. Len Williams was put up for the night in a hotel and the crew of both ships were all well treated. Seán O'Hegarty even seems to have apologised to the crew of the *Warrior* for the inconvenience he put them through. On the other hand, one has to acknowledge the terrible loss of life and destruction of property that ultimately resulted from the captured munitions.

CONCLUSION

After Ernest retired, he and Louise divided their time between London and the Riviera. They had plenty of opportunity for afternoon tea and tennis and they frequently attended receptions and garden parties at Buckingham Palace. Ernest also enjoyed golfing and he involved himself with numerous navy and colonial organisations, among them the Royal Navy Club and the Australian Natives Association, which promoted a 'white Australia'.

Their three children were growing up and doing well. Sheila's health improved considerably after she spent three years in Switzerland undergoing treatment for her 'brittle bone disease'. On her return to London Lady Louise presented her as a debutante to the king and queen at the palace.

Around this time, Louise's health took a turn for the worse. Sheila recalled: 'Then mother, never strong, became very ill. It was a terrible illness more mental than physical of course … There was a history of madness in her family. Servants would not stay and one day the doctors suggested to father that she be put away. Father looked at the doctors and said: 'Gentlemen I took the most solemn vows that man can take "for better or worse, in sickness and in health". Good day to you gentlemen'.

'So father and I nursed her, my brother [John] was in Africa, my sister [Yvonne] still a schoolgirl away at boarding school. She could never be left alone and sometimes I would fear father would break, because as so often happens in these cases she turned against him'.

From this description, Louise appears to have developed early onset or pre-senile dementia. Ernest brought her to the best doctors, but to no avail and finally she passed away in January 1934. They had been married thirty-five years. Sheila remembered: 'Eventually she died and we were distraught, both of us. I think looking back we were both exhausted … Three months after her death father took me around the world and then he was happiness all the way'. Even after she married Frederick de Moleyns – 'a marvellous man, very like father' – in 1936, she continued to accompany Ernest to dinners and other social occasions. Three years later Yvonne married Dick Fox a colonial administrator in the Gold Coast (now Ghana) in west Africa.

John moved to Southern Rhodesia in Africa, where he entered politics. Becoming a cabinet minister in the colonial administration and in 1965 playing a key role in the country's unilateral declaration of independence and the formation of a racist – apartheid-like – state under the premiership of Ian Smith. As a reward he was appointed ambassador to South Africa.

The lives of Ernest and Louise's children mirrored how inexorably connected to the empire they had been. Though now the sun was finally setting.

Towards the end of his life Ernest was diagnosed with cancer and in 1940 at the age of seventy-five he was admitted to Westminster Hospital in critical condition, where he was attended to by the king's physician Lord Horder. As he lay weak in his hospital bed he turned to Sheila: 'Sweetheart, I wonder what the *Times* will give me? Three paragraphs?'

The *Times* exceeded his dying question by printing a large obituary titled 'Great Fighting Career on Sea and Land', which included an extensive biography and a picture of him resplendent in uniform. It hailed him for 'a career of great distinction'. In Australia, the government ordered flags to be flown at half-mast. 'Nothing could have pleased my father more', remarked Sheila.

Gaunt's obituaries commemorated his many victories, accomplishments and displays of bravery. There was the time he battled a fierce storm off the Siberian coast, the charge he led at Durbo, Somalia, not to mention his brave and skilful leadership at Jutland. But strangely there wasn't any mention of the *Upnor*.

Throughout his career Ernest Gaunt faithfully served king, queen and empire. He worshiped the Royal Navy. He lived his life according to the principles he espoused: love of God, country and family. His beliefs on race and class have long since fallen out of favour and even in his own time they were fiercely contested.

He may not have been a superb admiral, but he was certainly a superb and brave captain. Above all he was a loyal and faithful husband and a wonderful, loving father.

After his resignation as brigade commander Seán O'Hegarty reportedly said to his friend Florence O'Donoghue: 'I'll go back to the poorhouse and I suppose you'll start selling collars again'. He returned to work as storekeeper at the South Infirmary Hospital, which was the successor to the old workhouse.

Following the Civil War he withdrew from politics and public life and never sought elected office. He limited his social life to a small circle of comrades and old friends and even amongst them refused to discuss the tragedy of the Civil War. When Míd died in 1940, he became 'an almost nightly visitor' to Florence O'Donoghue's home where the two would sit and chat over endless cups of tea.

Seán became a tireless advocate on behalf of the veterans of his brigade. He was particularly distraught about the excommunication of his fighters by Daniel Cohalan, the Catholic bishop of Cork, and spent years trying to reverse the edict. In 1930 he wrote to the Papal Nuncio (the pope's ambassador) in Dublin: 'the men are now scattered ... but wherever they are and under whatever conditions they live, over all our heads hovers the nightmare horror of this Decree of Excommunication: tarnishing our honour, besmirching our motives, a challenge to our historical justification, a menace to the salvation of our souls'. However his efforts were in vain.

Another cause he embraced was the repatriation of the remains of Father's Albert and Dominic back to Ireland for reburial; the pair had been exiled to America by the church for their support of the IRA. Seán was particularly close to Father Dominic who as brigade chaplain had given him a theological rationale for the IRA's campaign. Eventually in 1958 the caskets containing the remains of both priests were flown into Shannon Airport, where they were received by Seán and the Taoiseach Éamon de Valera and brought to Cork for re-internment, following requiem mass presided by

Bishop Lucey. It was a dignified and fitting tribute to two patriot priests.

Seán passed away in 1963 at the age of eighty-two at the Bon Secours Hospital in Cork. There was a large attendance at his funeral, headed by de Valera who was now president. A host of old comrades paid their respect including: Sandow, Mick Leahy, Tom Barry, Jim and Miah Gray, Frank Busteed, Margaret Lucey of Cumann na mBan, Florence O'Donoghue, Martin Corry, Dan Breen and one of the Wallace sisters (two unsung heroes of the revolution).

The *Cork Examiner* called him 'one of the foremost leaders in the fight for independence' adding 'in later years he never ceased to take an interest in the welfare of his old comrades'. Tom Barry had earlier written: 'His prestige with the Irish Republican Army was exceptionally high, not only as a result of his long years of national service, but because of his fine character, keen brain and personality. Honest, outspoken even to a fault, hating sham and pretence'. Praise from Barry was not easily earned.

Florence O'Donoghue wrote: 'To some he appeared a severe and formidable man, severe in his judgements, formidable in his intolerance of opinions which conflicted with his rigid principles, but those who knew him well will know that these were no more than some aspects of a fine, sensitive character in which was great warmth, great sincerity and great strength'.

Seán was never awarded the fine medals and titles that Ernest Gaunt received. He never attended a military academy. He probably never golfed or played tennis in his entire life and certainly he and Míd never owned a villa in Monte Carlo. But he was smarter, tougher and equally brave. Both Seán and Ernest were intolerant of opposing points of view and they both used and justified violence to achieve their goals. They were also both lonely people.

Seán made a massive and unappreciated contribution to the independence of Ireland and somewhat ironically to a democratic one. The one time in his life he decided to back down it was the right thing to do and he knew it. Forgotten or not, his legacy is still with us today.

NOTES AND REFERENCES

ABBREVIATIONS

ADM: Admiralty papers, NA
BL: British Library
BMH: Bureau of Military History, Military Archives, Dublin
CAB: Cabinet papers, NA
CAI: Cork Archives Institute
CHAR: Chartwell Trust, includes the papers of Winston Churchill, Cambridge
CO: Colonial Office papers, NA
FO: Foreign Office papers, NA
HO: Home Office papers, NA.
IWM: Imperial War Museum, London
MA: Military Archives, Dublin
NA: National Archives, Kew.
NAI: National Archives of Ireland
NLA: National Library of Australia.
NLI: National Library of Ireland
NPG: National Portrait Gallery, London.
UCDA: University College Dublin, Archives
WO: War Office papers, NA
WS: Witness statements (numbered) from the Bureau of Military History.

MAJOR REFERENCES

I have spent many years searching and accumulating information on the capture of the *Upnor* and the participants; in the course of which I visited numerous archives, libraries, museums and historical sites, corresponded with archivists and specialists by email and searched online.

The single most important archive was the National Archives in Kew where I read all the relevant documents I could find. Among the Admiralty papers were the official report on the capture of the *Upnor* and malicious damages claims (ADM 178/100), communications including telegrams to and from Queenstown and Admiral Gaunt (e.g. ADM 116/2135), documents on the naval facilities in Queenstown (e.g. ADM 239/15),

Ernest Gaunt's service records (ADM 196/88, 20 and 42) and numerous ships' logs. The Colonial Office papers contained correspondence and telegrams to and from Winston Churchill (CO 906/20) and minutes of meetings held at his office (CO 739/5). Gaunt's reports from South America and the South Pacific were found in the Foreign Office papers (FO 371/16 and FO 534/107). A comprehensive examination of the Queenstown harbour defences (WO 33/604) was among the War Office papers. The Cabinet Papers contained reports on the military situation in Ireland (CAB 24/136 and 23/30), many from General Macready. A report by Admiral Gaunt and General Macready (HO 317/61) and an assessment of the Sinn Féin leadership (HO 317/49) were among the Home Office papers.

In the Imperial War Museum I reviewed the papers and diary of General Sir Peter Strickland and documents from the 6th Division (which was headquartered in Cork), along with the papers of General Jeudwine and Field Marshal Sir Henry Wilson. At the Chartwell Trust, Cambridge I searched through the Churchill papers, including communications to and from Churchill (CHAR 22/11 and 22/12) and a situation report prepared by him for the cabinet (CHAR 22/12 A-B).

At the Cork Archives Institute the most important sources were the Liam de Róiste diaries and Connie Neenan's Memoirs. Cork County Library contains copies of the *Cork Examiner* and *Cork Constitution* from 1922. The University College Dublin Archives house the Ernie O'Malley papers and notebooks, especially interviews with Sandow O'Donovan (P 17b/95), Mick Leahy (P 17b/108), Tom Crofts (P 17b/108) and Mick Murphy (P 17b/111 and 112).

In Dublin the Military Archives at Cathal Brugha Barracks houses the Bureau of Military History witness statements, which are also available online. I read hundreds of the witness statements, the most relevant of which were: Michael Leahy WS 1,421, 94 and 555. Michael Burke WS 1,424. Seamus Fitzgerald WS 1,737. Daniel [Sandow] O'Donovan, WS 1,480. Michael Murphy, WS 1,547. Liam Deasy, WS 562. Donal Hales, WS 292. Dan Corkery, WS 1,719. Daniel Breen, WS 1,763. Leo Buckley, WS 1,714. Sean Culhane, WS 746. Seán Lucey, WS 1,579. Michael O'Donoghue, WS 1,741. Additionally I reviewed numerous Irish military service (1916–23) pension applications online.

There are also multiple valuable interviews in Uinseann MacEoin's book *Survivors*; including those with Tomás Ó Maoileóin, Seán McBride, Pax Ó Faoláin, Dan Gleeson, Tom Maguire and Peter Carleton.

I received considerable information and documentation from Dr John Borgonovo of University College Cork, whom I met several times and corresponded with online. Additionally his books and published articles were invaluable sources for this book.

Principal references for the capture of the *Upnor* and for the dialogue.
The following references were my principal sources for information specific to the actual seizure of the *Upnor* and the *Warrior*. They give an overview of the operation and are largely based on interviews with the participants,. They contain extensive dialogue. While they are all in substantive agreement, when it comes to details there are a number of discrepancies. Sandow appears to be a more reliable source than Mick Murphy, who was prone to exaggeration and boasting. There's a very useful map of the route taken by the *Upnor* and the *Warrior* in *The Sunday Press* article.

The Upnor file, ADM 178/100 in the National Archives, Kew. Bureau of Military History witness statements by: Michael Burke (WS 1,424) and Daniel [Sandow] O'Donovan (WS 1,480). Ernie O'Malley's interviews in the UCD Archives, with Sandow O'Donovan (P 17b/95), Mick Murphy (P 17b/111 and 112) and Mick Leahy (P 17b/108). Eoin Neeson's book *The Irish Civil War: 1922–23*, (pp. 97–100), which is an account of the operation from Sandow's perspective. Michael O'Halloran, 'The IRA Turned Pirates', based on an interview with Sandow O'Donovan in *The Sunday Press*, 6 December 1959. Liam Robinson, 'A Double Bluff Captures the Cruising Arsenal' based on an interview with Mick Murphy in *The Sunday Express*, 17 May 1959.

1. Medusa's Return

It seems unbelievable that Admiral Gaunt learned about the capture of the *Warrior* from a newspaper. However, at the beginning of the navy's inquiry into the incident he stated that's indeed what happened (ADM 178/100): 'In the morning paper of the 30th of March I read the following report as to the sailing of the Warrior'. There then follows a clipping from the *Cork Constitution* with the heading 'HMS Medusa' and an account of his frantic efforts to search for the *Warrior* and the *Upnor*.

2: Tremble and Obey

I was able to glean considerable understanding of Gaunt's personality, beliefs and family life from his letters (in the British Library and National Library of Australia), his reports and service records in the National Archives, books by his sister Mary and brother Guy and above all from the recording of his daughter Sheila de Moleyn's talk (May 1980, in the Liddle Collection, University of Leeds) about him.

Early in his career, Ernest wrote a poem in praise of the modern navy:

> Our sails are all gone, and instead we have now
> A screw sticking out on each quarter;
> Grape, canister, chain we have none of these shot,
> But Maxims will add to the slaughter.
> And better than all we have moved with the times...
> Our bluejackets [sailors] hearts are of steel not of oak,
> They've followed the ships in their changes

Though lacking any literary merit these juvenile verses reflected his enthusiasm for the navy and the Maxim machine gun, the latter of which he went on to use with considerable effect. Reference: EFAG. 'Navy Changes', *United Service Magazine*, IX (May 1894), p. 104

3: A Ruthless Bastard

Since the Coolnacaheragh ambush was an intense firefight, witnesses differ in the details of the events. However, by analysing and cross-referencing the evidence, I've endeavoured to provide a reliable and accurate account.

In the description of 'Hegarty's crowd' I've paraphrased a sentence from Peter Hart's *The IRA and its Enemies* (pp. 240–1).

Despite the lack of documentation on Seán's personal life, some insight can be gained from Kevin Girvin's biography, *Seán O'Hegarty: Officer Commanding, First Cork Brigade, Irish Republican Army*, comments by his close friend and comrade Florence O'Donoghue, especially in *Florence and Josephine O'Donoghue's War* and the transcript of a speech by Seán in *The Youghal Tribune*, 10 Aug. 1946.

Sandow's full quote about O'Hegarty was: 'he was a ruthless bastard and nothing would stop him', from Sandow's interview in the, O'Malley Notebooks, P 17b/95, UCDA. To be called 'ruthless' by Sandow was akin to being called 'smart' by Albert Einstein.

5: Micky and Dicky

Quote from John Borgonovo about Michael Collins' and GHQ's lack of support of the IRA's country units in *Florence and Josephine O'Donoghue's War* (p. 106).

In *For the Life of Me* Robert Briscoe who oversaw the smuggling of the Luger parabellums into Cork likely significantly exaggerated the size of the shipment and the number was probably substantially less than 200.

James Stephens wrote a poem, the *Ould Snarly Gob* (1909), about a bitter and lonely old man whose only comfort was to take pleasure in the pain of others.

6: The Italian Job

Mick Leahy expressed deep dissatisfaction with Collins and the GHQ staff in his interview with Ernie O'Malley and in his BMH witness statement. I have included three paragraphs of quoted text which detail Leahy's trip to Dublin. The first two paragraphs are from his witness statement and the third paragraph is from his interview with O'Malley. Tom Cullen was the assistant director of intelligence and the quartermaster-general at GHQ.

Before Mick Leahy went to Genoa, several Sinn Féin and IRA emissaries made contact with Italian government officials, army officers and right wing militants. British intelligence was aware of at least some of these activities, though not fully informed about Leahy's plans. For the sake of brevity I have omitted many of the details of the meetings prior to Leahy's arrival.

Mark Phelan wrote an excellent article about this operation in *History Ireland*: 'Gabriele D'Annunzio and the Irish Republic' (issue 5, Sept./Oct. 2013, vol. 21). There are also multiple accounts in the BMH witness statements: Michael Leahy (WS 555), Donal Hales (WS 292), Florence O'Donoghue (WS 554), Liam Deasy (WS 562), Liam O'Briain (WS 565), Seán Ó Seaghdha (WS 760) and P. J. Paul (WS 877). See also Report by General Macready on the situation in Ireland, week ending April 2, 1922 (CAB, 24/121, NA).

Liam Deasy wrote (*Towards Ireland Free*, p. 179) that he planned to have the *Stella Maris* beached near Myross and then unloaded. However, Mick Leahy (Bureau of Military History, WS 555, p. 2), who was considerably more authoritative on nautical matters, stated that 'there was no question of beaching the ship' and this is supported by Patrick O'Driscoll (WS 557). Additionally O'Driscoll wrote that the cargo was to be transferred offshore into a large trawler, which would then anchor inside of Rabbit Island. I'm unable to verify this plan which seems overly complex and risky.

7: Queenstown, 1921

I visited Admiralty House on two occasions and was able to stand out on the balcony and look out to sea as Admiral Gaunt once did. Additionally I saw Admiral and Lady Gaunt's guest books, which were signed by visitors to the house.

The current Rob Roy Bar is significantly smaller than the Rob Roy Hotel that existed in 1922.

Admiral Gaunt's quotations are taken from the lecture by his daughter Sheila de Moleyns. The so called 'cannibal' island was likely in Fiji, which Louise and Ernest visited during his command of *HMS Cambrian*. Montgomery, renowned for his rudeness and inflated ego, was nearly killed in 1922 by O'Hegarty's brigade in Macroom. He went on to become Britain's most feted general in the Second World War.

Kieran McCarthy in his book *Republican Cobh and the East Cork Volunteers Since 1913* describes in great detail the IRA activities in Queenstown and the surrounding countryside.

Mick Burke's attack against the warships was a notable success, however in his BMH witness statement (WS 1,424) he exaggerated the extent of damage and though all the vessels took on water not all of them sank.

It's possible that Mick Murphy's intended target when he set up the ambush at the Marino in Cork was General Strickland rather than Gaunt, despite what Laurence Neville (a member of his battalion) said in his BMH statement (WS 1,639).

During the Battle of Jutland Prince Albert served on the battleship *Collingwood*, which was part of Gaunt's division.

8: The Cork Republic

The Cork Republic has also been called the 'Munster Republic'.

Under the terms of the Treaty Cork Harbour was classified as a 'treaty port' granting the Royal Navy continued access and the British retaining responsibility for the harbour defences, including Spike Island.

Regarding the kidnapping of Arthur Kay, I've disregarded obvious exaggerations and inaccuracies in F.W. Memory's book, *"Memory's": Being the adventures of a Newspaperman*. It's extremely interesting that Kay was able to accurately describe the actual conditions at Knockraha prison, despite this only becoming well known in recent decades. Whoever threatened him was well aware as to what was going on.

9: De Courcy

I have been unable to definitively identify who the IRA informant was. Sandow in his interview with Ernie O'Malley and in his BMH witness statement gave his name as 'de Courcy', a member of C Company, 1st Battalion. Though when Sandow was interviewed for a newspaper a few years later the name was written as 'de Lourey' which could have been a typographic error. Connie Neenan identifies the informant's company and battalion but doesn't give his name. I searched the BMH, witness statements and the Military Archive's pension applications but was unable to find a 'de Courcy', 'de Lourey' 'Loury' or any other similar name which would match. McCarthy in his book on the Cobh IRA gave his name as 'Delourey'.

Leahy in his interview with O'Malley said that the informant was 'Alec Sullivan' There is information about an IRA informant in Cobh of that name, though whether he was the source of information on the *Upnor* is uncertain. Leahy's involvement in the capture of the *Upnor* was much less central than that of Sandow, though on the other hand Sandow might have been trying to conceal the informant's name. For further information on 'De Courcy' see: Sandow O'Donovan, P 17b/95, O'Malley Notebooks, UCDA. Mick Murphy, P 17b/112, O'Malley Notebooks, UCDA. Connie Neenan. Memoirs, p. 44, CAI. Daniel O'Donovan, WS 1,480, BMH, p. 1. *Sunday Press*, 6 December 1959. Mick Leahy, P 17b/108, O'Malley Notebooks, UCDA.

The All for Ireland Club at Emmet Place (together with the neighbouring premises at number 5) is now a Costa Coffee shop. The leader of the All for Ireland League, William O'Brien was from Mallow in Cork, later he became sympathetic to Sinn Féin and went on to oppose the Treaty. He was in contact with members of O'Hegarty's brigade, see Tom Crofts, P 17b/108, O'Malley Notebooks, UCDA.

There were likely several planning meetings and though I do not have details of these, I have taken an account of O'Hegarty leading a brigade council from Sean O'Callaghan's book Execution. Additionally Seán Healy in WS 1,479 gave a description of how O'Hegarty recruited him for a hazardous special operation. The words attributed to O'Hegarty here are based on inference. Mick Leahy, in his interview with O'Malley, took considerable credit for the plan, however I have been unable to collaborate this. The account in Eoin Neeson's book on the Irish Civil War about the capture of the Upnor appears to be largely based on interviews with Sandow O'Donovan.

The book *Decoding the IRA* by Thomas Mahon and James Gillogly, which is based on top secret IRA communications, gives considerable insight into the personality of Sandow, who went by the pseudonym 'Mr Jones' when conducting intelligence work in the United States and spying for the Russians after the Civil War.

According to Sandow in *Green Tears for Hecuba*, Con O'Sullivan panicked during the shooting of Col Smyth and afterwards suffered from post-traumatic stress disorder. Though I haven't been able to verify this.

10: The Ball at their Feet
Connie Neenan wrote in his memoirs that during the Army Convention O'Hegarty supported the idea of a dictatorship, while Liam de Róiste who was not there, but is a highly reliable source, wrote: 'Seán O'Hegarty

opposed the idea of the dictatorship'. De Róiste's statement would fit with O'Hegarty's later stance. O'Hegarty returned from the convention in a car that accompanied the *River Lee*. The armoured car later saw action in the Civil War.

From Sandow's interview with Ernie O'Malley it appears that Peter O'Donovan wasn't initially picked to be part of the team to capture the *Upnor*. In this account Sandow asked him not to go to the convention but to stay behind and to send a telegram to Dublin if the *Upnor* appeared ready to sail so that they could rush back. O'Donovan agreed, but on condition that he could join the team.

12: A Speedy Departure

The family of Capt. Collins believe that his kidnapping was 'staged' to furnish him with an alibi and that also he was involved in the planning of the operation from the start. While I respect their position and acknowledge that his role was indispensable I found no evidence of this in my research. It was O'Hegarty's policy to never share operational information with people who weren't part of his inner circle or members of the IRB. Furthermore, numerous accounts state that the captain had no advance knowledge, these include: Mick Murphy's interviews in the O'Malley Notebooks and in the *Sunday Express*, Sandow's interviews in the O'Malley notebooks, the *Sunday Press* and his BMH witness statement, Mick Burke's witness statement, statements by Charles Regan and Charles Parker of the *Warrior* in ADM 178/100 and Eoin Neeson's book on the Civil War.

I don't know precisely where Capt. Collins' bank was, but it was most likely on the South Mall. *The Times* simply states that he was 'kidnapped outside a bank in Cork'.

I've used the name 'Cobh' in this section, as Seán O'Hegarty and his comrades would have called the town either this or 'Cove', which was the original name.

I don't know what Seán O'Hegarty actually said to Sandow and Mick Murphy as they left to kidnap Capt. Collins, but based on his comments in other situations I expect him to have made a terse, sarcastic remark to hide his concern.

The brigade had a number of cars. Jim Grey's favourite seems to have been the red Buick, but they also had a Hupmobile and most likely the Rolls Royce that was commandeered in Dublin for the kidnapping of Arthur Kay. While I'm uncertain as to which car each group travelled in, it's more likely that the larger contingent travelled in the seven seater Buick. In those days petrol was carried in tin cans since the first petrol station in Ireland didn't open until 1923.

Since Sandow and Murphy walked to Rushbrooke from the Deepwater Quay there must have been no cars at the quay when the *Hellespont* failed to dock as expected. Therefore the second car likely left to drop off Buckley or to return to Cork. I'm uncertain as to what Sandow actually said to Mick Burke, however he was known for his colourful language. It's unclear why Leahy never met the driver sent to collect him, perhaps for once in his life he was too frightened. In his BMH witness statement Sandow merely stated 'for some unknown reason he did not turn up'.

There are minor discrepancies from witnesses on the sequence of events after the IRA boarded the tug, most likely as a result of things unfolding extremely quickly. I don't know for sure what Sandow said to Duhig. As they passed the British forts, Sandow and Collins remained on the bridge, while the others hid out of sight.

According to Mick Leahy a warship escorted the *Upnor* as far as the harbour mouth. But this is uncollaborated by other sources, including the navy. Furthermore Leahy is an unreliable witness for this operation. 'Any ship that left Haulbowline they sent a destroyer escort with it so we thought they would do the same with this boat … The destroyer turned back and it met the *Warrior* as it was on its way out to sea', Leahy, P 17b/108, O'Malley Notebooks, UCDA.

Sandow stated that he went to Horne's office along with Burke and another Cobh volunteer. Mick Murphy does not appear to have been part of this group, although curiously Burke wrote that he and Murphy talked about what they should do with Horne after they captured him.

13: The Ballycotton Convoy

Estimates of the size convoy vary. The *Cork Constitution* wrote initially that it consisted of twenty to thirty lorries, but then corrected itself to say 'one hundred vehicles'. *The Irish Times* wrote that there were 100 motor cars and lorries, while Mick Murphy said 200. The most accurate account is probably Sandow's, who told Ernie O'Malley that there were seventy-five. This comes close to Connie Neenan's estimate of eighty lorries and four steam lorries. Neenan also mentioned the presence of at least one motorbike. The numbers I have given are quoted from Neeson's book, who appears to have used Sandow as his source. The story about the steam roller is most likely an example of Cork humour.

I don't know exactly where the lorries were formed into a convoy, but Glanmire, just beyond Victoria Barracks and on the road to Ballycotton would have been a good location. Mick Murphy said that the convoy was assembled halfway between Cork and Ballycotton, which would seem to be too far from the city. Additionally Murphy's information on the convoy was based on hearsay. I've no information as to how Leahy eventually got to Ballycotton or what excuse he gave to O'Hegarty for his earlier absence, but the fact is that he did eventually turn up there.

De Róiste used the term 'Bolshevik' for any faction whom he held responsible for the breakdown in law and order and who were preventing the Provisional Government establishing its authority.

14: Message from the Admiralty

Throughout the operation the actions and frequently the words of Sandow, Murphy, Capt. Collins, Capt. Hoar and the crew of the *Warrior* and to a lesser extent those of Burke, O'Hegarty and Leahy are documented by multiple sources, but the role of other participants is largely unknown.

The IRA members never revealed their real names to the crews of the *Upnor* and *Warrior*. For instance Murphy, and most likely also Sandow, was addressed as 'commandant' in front of the prisoners. The term 'chief' seems to have been reserved for O'Hegarty.

The references quote considerable dialogue between Collins and the IRA. Capt. Collins told the *Warrior's* mate and Able Seaman Regan that he had been kidnapped by the IRA, again this was likely with a view to protecting himself and his businesses from retribution by the British or the Provisional Government.

The *Upnor's* flag is now at Cork Public Museum. The King's Harbour Master's flag strongly resembled a Pilot Jack – used by harbour pilots – which is what the first mate on the *Upnor* confused it for. Mick Burke in his witness statement was mistaken when he said that the *Upnor* was escorted by two armed Royal Navy drifters. Mick Murphy in his interview with O'Malley described the envelope they brought with them as a 'hell of a big envelope'. Capt. Hoar stated that the *Upnor* was boarded thirty [nautical] miles S.S.E. of Roches Point at 6:30 p.m. Hoar also reported his revolver was a Smith and Wesson, therefore Murphy who later recalled it as a Webley was likely mistaken.

The map printed in the *Sunday Press* shows the ships sailing around and outside of Ballycotton Island, which would have been the safest route to the pier. The fifteen metre high Ballycotton Lighthouse is one of only three lighthouses in the world painted black; the others being in Texas and Australia. This was done to distinguish it from the nearby (and never completed) Capel Island Lighthouse.

Sailing/harbours/Ballycotton, accessed 8 June 2020 (eoceanic.com/sailing/harbours/32/ballycotton) gives an excellent account of the geography of Ballycotton Bay from a nautical perspective.

Sandow wrote in his witness statement: 'when the approach of the ships was reported the whole party moved into Ballycotton with the transport, to await the arrival of the *Warrior* and *Upnor*'. Therefore they must have been waiting somewhere just north of the village.

The IRA had Very guns and this would have been the most efficient way for the scouts to have signalled to O'Hegarty in the dark. Seán brought the lorries, five or so at a time, onto the pier to avoid a bottleneck. Therefore the other trucks would have been parked nearby. I'm unsure as to where exactly, however the fork in the road is one hundred metres from the pier and would have been an ideal location where they could turn around and wait their turn.

15: The Fecking War is Over

The title of this chapter comes from Mick Leahy quoting Mick Murphy, in his interview with Ernie O'Malley (P 17b/108). Leahy said that a local pilot by the name of Reardon piloted the *Upnor* into the harbour. Therefore it's likely that he led the way and that the *Warrior* followed. Ballycotton was a small fishing harbour and therefore the pier likely had mooring rings rather than bollards, which were used by larger vessels. As soon as the *Upnor* docked the crew were ordered ashore and then allowed to return. Murphy may have been initially concerned that if the crew stayed on the ship they could have attempted to disrupt the unloading.

Following the IRA's consolidation of power in Cork in 1922 Seán O'Hegarty had considerable money at his disposal, which would have allowed him to distribute such cheques. On the other hand much of Gaunt's information was unreliable and so this may or may not be true. Charles Regan said that he was given a £1 Treasury note for the whiskey.

I have paraphrased the paragraph on the IRA telephone operator from the *Sunday Press* article.

My estimates of the quantity of munitions captured are based largely on government and admiralty documents kept at the National Archives in Kew and at the Churchill Archives, including the Admiralty Report on the Seizure of the *Upnor*, as well as naval telegrams and records from the Colonial Office. Additionally I have reviewed evidence from IRA sources, including statements by Sandow O'Donovan and Mick Burke. The sources include telegrams from Gaunt to Admiralty, 30 and 31 March and 3 April 1922, *Upnor* file, ADM 178/100 and Irish Telegrams, January to June 1922, CO 906/20, NA. Conference called by Churchill, 31 March 1922, CO 906/20, NA. *Sunday Press*, 6 December 1959. Eoin Neeson, *Irish Civil War*, p. 100. Neenan. Memoirs, 44, CAI. C-in-c Devonport, 1 April 1922, CHAR 22/12. Minutes of a conference held in the Secretary of State's Room, 3 April 1922, CO 739/5, NA. Macready to C.I.G.S. 3 April, 1922, WO 23/9530, NA. Churchill in the Commons, British Tug Piratical seizure, 3 and 5 April 1922, Hansard. Admiralty to Under Secretary of State, 5

April 1922, CO 739/5, NA. Telegram received in Irish Office from Cope, 5 April 1922, CO 739/5, NA. List of armament stores deficient, *Upnor* file, June 1922, ADM 178/100, NA. The following Bureau of Military History statements: Michael Burke (WS 1,424, pp. 34–6). Patrick McHugh (WS 664). Daniel O'Donovan (WS 1,480). Maurice Brew (WS 1,695). John Regan, *Irish Counter-Revolution*, pp. 114–5. Florence O'Donoghue, *No Other Law*, p. 226. Mick Murphy, P 17b/112, O'Malley Notebooks, UCDA. 6th Battalion, IRA Report, April to July 1922, photocopy given to me by John Borgonovo.

16: Hitting the Fan

Gaunt realised that the *Upnor* was in danger at around 10:00 in the morning, since he sent the first telegram – that I've managed to find – concerning the search at 10:27. Gaunt interrogated Len Williams in person, however, most if not all of his communication with Horne appears to have been by telegram or letter.

Macready's quote in full is 'Even in the old days of the Agadir business and the Declaration of War in '14 was as nothing to the wild excitement consequent on the capture by Mr. Barry of one of His Majesty's ships of war', from Macready to Wilson, 6 April 1922, Papers of Henry Wilson, IWM. The Agadir Crisis of 1911 was a dispute between France and Germany over the colonisation of Morocco, which nearly precipitated a European War.

The official transcripts of debates in the House of Commons are published by Hansard, hansard.millbanksystems.com/commons

The minutes of a meeting held between British representatives, including Macready, and Michael Collins and his associates state: 'The Provisional Government's representatives were much concerned at the capture at Cork [of the *Upnor*] ... and apparently did not believe the figures given by Mr. Churchill in the House' (Meeting held at the Headquarters of the PG, 4 April 1922, CO 739/11, NA).

Information on the malicious damages claims by the British government is available in the official admiralty report on the *Upnor* (ADM 178/100) along with documents from the National Archives of Ireland sent to me by Chris White of Historical RFA (Royal Fleet Auxiliary) website.

A good example of how out of touch Gaunt was is contained in a telegram he sent on 6 April to the Admiralty: 'Secret informer states Free Staters were in *Upnor* seizure with Republicans. Coup in preparation is probably declaration of Republic Easter week.'

On the occasion that Ernest was invested, Gen. Strickland also received a KBE, while Macready was made a baronet, which was a much more prestigious and a heritable honour.

In June 1922 a Royal Navy captain reported: 'A republican general lives in Admiralty House over which fly the republican colours', which was most likely a reference to Mick Burke.

17: Civil War

Mick Leahy recalled Mick Murphy's reaction to the death of Michael Collins in his interview with Ernie O'Malley (P 17b/108).

John Brennan a senior civil servant with the Department of Finance in Dublin wrote to his counterparts in London that: 'the successful plunder [of the *Upnor*] by the Irregulars was a factor of importance in enabling the latter during subsequent months to offer violent resistance to the government... with all the unfortunate consequences' (letter from Brennan, n.d., Malicious Damages Claims in ADM 178/100, NA.).

John Duhig along with Seumas Robinson burned Tipperary creamery, though Tom Crofts reported that he and Liam Deasy were 'annoyed' since the local farmers – 'our people' – suffered economic hardship as there was nowhere to sell their milk to. In the interview Crofts also discussed the serious and lasting economic consequences of the destruction of the Mallow viaduct. (Crofts, P 17b/108, O'Malley Notebooks, UCDA).

John Borgonovo wrote in an e-mail to me: 'Accounts of the early fighting in the Civil War make it clear that the Cork IRA were using machine guns freely' (15 November 2010).

Neeson in *The Irish Civil War* (100) echoed Florence O'Donoghue's statement that the *Upnor* haul was the largest of only three significant caches obtained by the Republicans in the south of Ireland (1st Southern Division) before the outbreak of the Civil War.

Admiralty House was gutted after the Republicans set fire to it in August 1922. Afterwards it was acquired by Bishop Browne and converted into Saint Benedict's Priory.

Conclusion

An example of how Seán's significance has been largely forgotten, unappreciated and ignored is that he does not even merit an entry in *A Biographical Dictionary of Cork* by Tim Cadogan and Jeremiah Falvey.

BIBLIOGRAPHY

Archival Sources

Cambridge
Churchill Archives Centre
Chartwell Trust Papers
Nicholas O'Conor papers

Canberra
National Library of Australia
Edmund Barton papers
Alfred Deakin papers

Chippenham
Wiltshire and Swindon History Centre
Walter Long papers

Cork
Cork City and County Archives
Connie Neenan memoirs
Liam de Róiste diaries
Riobárd Langford papers
Cork City Library
Cork Constitution and *Cork Examiner* newspaper archives
Customs House
Cork Harbour Commissioners Meeting Minutes

Dublin
Met Éireann
National Library of Ireland
Florence O'Donoghue papers.
University College Dublin Archives
Ernie O'Malley papers and notebooks

Leeds
University of Leeds
Liddle Collection

London
British Library
Admiral Jellicoe papers

Imperial War Museum
General Strickland Papers
Field Marshal Wilson Papers
General Jeudwine Papers
National Archives
Admiralty Papers
Cabinet Papers
Colonial Office Papers
Foreign Office Papers
Home Office Papers
War Office Papers
National Portrait Gallery
Admiral Gaunt
Lady Gaunt

Sydney
State Library of New South Wales, Mitchell Library
HMS Cambrian album of photographs

Journals and Periodicals
Admiral and Lady Gaunt's Guest Books, courtesy of the nuns of Saint
    Benedict's Priory, Cobh
The Capuchin Annual
An Cosanthóir
Engineering
The Fourth Estate
Harper's Monthly Magazine
History Ireland
International Journal of Maritime History
Irish Geography
Irish Historical Studies
The Irish Sword
The Journal of Modern History
The Journal of the Royal Historical and Archaeological Association of Ireland
The Lawrence Collection: Images of Queenstown/Cobh: 1865–1914. 2015
    calendar
The Marine Engineer
The Melbournian
The Naval Annual
The Naval Review
United Service Magazine

The 79th News (paper of the Cameron Highlanders Regiment)

Newspapers

Ireland
Cork Constitution
Cork Examiner
Freeman's Journal
Irish Independent
Irish Times
Southern Star
Sunday Press
Youghal Tribune

Britain
The Times
Bath Chronicle and Weekly Gazette
Daily Express
Daily Mail
Derby Daily Telegraph
Edinburgh Evening News
Evening Telegraph
Hampshire Telegraph and Sussex Chronicle
Hull Daily Mail
Manchester Courier
Manchester Courier and Lancashire General Advertiser
Pall Mall Gazette
Sheffield Daily Telegraph
Sunday Express
Western Times (Exeter)
Worcestershire Chronicle

Australia and New Zealand
Advertiser (Adelaide)
Argus (Melbourne)
Brisbane Courier
Clarence and Richmond Examiner (New South Wales)
Evening Post (Wellington)
Examiner (Tasmania)
Mail (Adelaide)
Mercury (Hobart)
Morning Bulletin (Queensland)
Otago Witness

Register (Adelaide)
Star (New Zealand)
Sunday Times (Perth)
Sydney Morning Herald

Rest of World
New York Times
New York Tribune
The Straits Times (Singapore)

Web sites
Clyde Maritime, clydemaritimeforums.co.uk
Daily Weather Reports, Met Office Digital Library and Archive, *digital. nmla.metoffice.gov.uk*
Dowling, A. *Gaunt, William Henry.* Australian Dictionary of Biography, online edition
The Diaries of Admiral George King-Hall, *kinghallconnections* on google. com
Bureau of Military History Witness Statements and Military Service Pension applications, militaryarchives.ie
Hansard, hansard.millbanksystems.com/commons
Historical RFA
British Pathé, on ifiplayer.ie
Sailing/harbours/Ballycotton, on eoceanic.com/sailing/harbours/32/bally cotton

Audio recording
De Moleyns, Sheila. Lecture on her father, Admiral Gaunt. Tape recording, May 1980. Liddle Collection, University of Leeds

Books
Abbott, Richard. *Police Casualties in Ireland, 1919–1922* (Mercier Press, Cork, 2000)
Andrews, C.S. *Dublin Made Me: An Autobiography* (Mercier Press, Dublin and Cork, 1979)
Augusteijn, Joost. *From Public Defiance to Guerrilla Warfare: The Experience of Ordinary Volunteers in the Irish War of Independence, 1916–1921* (Irish Academic Press, Dublin, 1996)
Battle of Jutland, 30ᵗʰ May to 1ˢᵗ June, 1916. Official dispatches with appendices (His Majesty's Stationary Office, London, 1920)
Barry, Dr. J.M. *Queenstown for Orders* (Sidney Publishing, Cork, 1999)
Barry, Tom. *Guerrilla Days in Ireland* (Anvil Books, Tralee, 1971). Reprinted by Mercier Press

Bartlett, Thomas and Jeffrey, Keith (eds.). *A Military History of Ireland* (Cambridge University Press, Cambridge, 1996)

Bayly, Admiral Sir Lewis. *Pull Together: The Memoirs of Admiral Sir Lewis Bayly* (George G. Harrap & Co, London, 1939)

Borgonovo, John. *Florence and Josephine O'Donoghue's War of Independence* (Dublin, Irish Academic Press, 2006)

—— *The Battle for Cork: July-August 1922* (Mercier Press, Cork, 2011)

—— *The Dynamics of War and Revolution: Cork City, 1916–1918* (Cork University Press, Cork, 2013)

—— *Spies, Informers and the 'Anti-Sinn Féin Society: The Intelligence War in Cork City, 1920–1921* (Irish Academic Press, Dublin, 2007)

Boyne, Seán. *Emmet Dalton: Somme Soldier, Irish General, Film Pioneer* (Merrion Press, Dublin, 2014)

Bowyer Bell, J. *The Secret Army: The IRA, 1916–1970* (The John Day Company, New York, 1971)

Brassey T. ed. *The Naval Annual 1905* (Portsmouth, 1905)

Briscoe, Robert. *For the Life of Me* (Little, Brown and Company, Boston, 1958)

Broderick, Mary. *History of Cobh (Queenstown) Ireland* (no publisher named, 1994)

Brunicardi, Niall. *Haulbowline, Spike and Rocky Islands* (Éigse Books, Fermoy, 1982)

Burke, John and Burke, John B. *Genealogical and Heraldic Dictionary of the Landed Gentry of Great Britain and Ireland* (Henry Colburn, London, 1847)

Burt, R.A. *British Battleships: 1889–1904* (Naval Institute Press, Annapolis, 2013)

Burt, R. A. *British Battleships of World War One* (Seaforth Publishing, Barnsley, 2012)

Cadogan, Tim. *Cobh in Old Picture Postcards* (Europese Bibliotheek, Netherlands, 1995)

—— *Cork in Old Photographs* (Gill & Macmillan, Dublin, 2003)

Cadogan, Tim and Falvey, Jeremiah. *A Biographical Dictionary of Cork* (Four Courts Press, Dublin, 2006)

Chatterton, E. Keble, *Danger Zone: The Story of the Queenstown Command* (Little, Brown and Company, Boston, 1934)

Chavesse, Moirin. *Terence MacSwiney* (Clonmore and Reynolds, Dublin, 1961)

Coogan, Tim Pat. *Eamon De Valera: The Man Who Was Ireland* (Harper Perennial, New York, 1996)

—— *Michael Collins: The Man Who Made Ireland* (Palgrave Macmillan,

London, 2002)

Costello, Francis. *The Irish Revolution and its Aftermath: 1916–1923* (Irish Academic Press, Dublin, 2003)

Cottrell, Peter (ed.). *The War for Ireland: 1913–1923* (Osprey Publishing, Oxford, 2009)

Cronin, Tom. *Cork: Then and Now* (The History Press Ireland, Dublin, 2012)

Crowley, John *et al* (eds). *Atlas of Cork City* (Cork University Press, Cork, 2005)

Crowley, John, Ó Drisceoil, Donal, Murphy, Mike and Borgonovo, John (eds.), *Atlas of the Irish Revolution* (Cork University Press, Cork, 2017)

Curtis, Keiron. *P. S. O'Hegarty (1879–1955): Sinn Féin Fenian* (Anthem Press, London, 2012)

Deasy, Liam. *Brother Against Brother* (Mercier Press, Cork, 1998)

— *Towards Ireland Free: The West Cork Brigade in the War of Independence 1917–21* (Royal Carbery Books, Cork, 1973)

Delano, Anthony. *Guy Gaunt: The Boy from Ballarat who Talked America into the Great War* (Arcadia, North Melbourne, 2017)

Doherty, Gabriel and Keogh, Dermot (eds). *Michael Collins and the Making of the Irish State* (Mercier Press, Cork, 1998)

Doherty, Gabriel (introduction). *With the IRA in the Fight for Freedom: 1919 to the Truce* (Cork, Mercier Press, 2010)

Dolan, Anne. *Commemorating the Irish Civil War: History and Memory, 1923–2000* (Cambridge University Press, Cambridge, 2003)

Doorley, Michael. *Irish-American Diaspora Nationalism: The Friends of Irish Freedom, 1916–1935* (Four Courts Press, Dublin, 2005)

Dougherty, Martin J. *Small Arms Visual Encyclopedia* (Amber Books, London, 2011)

Fallon, Charlotte H. *Soul of Fire: A Biography of Mary MacSwiney* (Mercier Press, Cork, 1986)

Fanning, Ronan. *Fatal Path: British Government and Irish Revolution: 1910–1922* (Faber and Faber, London, 2013)

Fawcett, H. and Hooper, G. *The Fighting at Jutland: The Personal Experiences of 45 Officers and Men of the British Fleet* (Macmillan and Co. London, 1921)

Feehan, John M. *The Shooting of Michael Collins: Murder or Accident?* (Royal Carbery Books, Cork, 1991)

Fitzpatrick, David. *Harry Boland's Irish Revolution* (Cork University Press, Cork, 2003)

— *Politics and Irish Life, 1913–1921: Provincial Experience of War and*

Revolution (Cork University Press, Cork, 1998)

Flanagan, Frank. *Reminiscences of 'The Pope' Flanagan* (Published by Richard Humphreys, Dublin, 2010)

Foster, R.F. *Vivid Faces: The Revolutionary Generation in Ireland, 1890–1923* (W.W. Norton and Company, New York, 2015)

Friedman, Norman. *British Cruisers of the Victorian Era* (Naval Institute Press, Annapolis, 2012)

Garner, William. *Cobh Architectural Heritage* (An Foras Forbartha, Dublin, 1979)

Gaughan, Anthony J. *Memoirs of Constable Jeremiah Mee, RIC* (Anvil Books, Dublin, 1975). Reprinted by Mercier Press

Gaunt, Guy. *The Yield of the Years* (Hutchinson, London, 1940)

Gaunt, Mary. *A Broken Journey* (T. Werner Laurie, London, 1919)

— *Alone in West Africa* (T. W. Laurie, London, 1918)

Girvin, Kevin. *Seán O'Hegarty: Officer Commanding, First Cork Brigade, Irish Republican Army* (Aubane Historical Society, Millstreet, 2007)

Gordon, Andrew. *The Rules of the Game: Jutland and British Naval Command* (Naval Institute Press, Annapolis, 2012)

Guys Cork Almanac and Directory, 1921 (Guy's and Co., Cork)

Guys Cork Almanac and Directory, 1930 (Guy's and Co., Cork)

Hart, Peter (ed.). *British Intelligence in Ireland, 1920–21: The Final Reports* (Cork University Press, Cork, 2002)

— *The IRA and its Enemies: Violence and Community in Cork, 1916–1923* (Clarendon Press, Oxford, 1998)

— *Mick: The Real Michael Collins* (Macmillan, London, 2005)

— (introduction). *Rebel Cork's Fighting Story 1916–21: Told by the Men Who Made It* (Cork, Mercier Press, 2010)

Harvey, Dan and White, Gerry. *The Barracks: A History of Victoria Barracks/Collins Barracks, Cork* (Mercier Press, Cork, 1997)

Herman, A. *To Rule the Waves: How the British Navy Shaped the Modern World* (Hodder, London, 2005)

Hill, J. R. (ed.), *A New History of Ireland: 1921–1984, Volume 7* (Oxford University Press, Oxford, 2010)

Hittle, J. B. E. *Michael Collins and the Anglo-Irish War* (Potomac Books, Washington D.C., 2011)

Hopkinson, Michael. *Green Against Green: The Irish Civil War* (Gill and Macmillan, Dublin, 1988)

— *The Irish War of Independence* (Dublin, Gill and Macmillan Ltd. 2002)

— (ed.). *The Last Days of Dublin Castle: The Mark Sturgis Diaries* (Irish Academic Press, Dublin, 1999)

Hydrographic Office US Navy. *Red Sea and Gulf of Aden Pilot*

(Government Printing Office, Washington DC, 1922)

Jeffries, Henry Alan. *Cork Historical Perspectives* (Four Courts Press, Dublin, 2004)

Kautt, W H. *Ambushes and Armour: The Irish Rebellion, 1919–1921* (Irish Academic Press, Dublin, 2010)

Lang, R.T. *Black's Guide to Ireland* (Adam and Charles Black, London, 1906)

Leabhar na hÉireann: The Irish Year Book, 1908 (James Duffy & Co, Dublin, 1908)

Lee, J.J. *Ireland 1912–1985: Politics and Society* (Cambridge University Press, Cambridge, 1993)

Lenihan, Michael. *Cork Burning* (Mercier Press, Cork, 2018)

—— *Timeless Cork* (Mercier Press, Cork, 2013)

Linton Bogle, James M.D., *The Meanderings of a Medico: A Record of Work and Travel in Many Lands* (Printed for Private Circulation, 1928)

London, Jack. *The Cruise of the Snark* (The Macmillan Company, New York 1914)

MacEoin, Uinseann. *Survivors* (Argenta Publications, Dublin, 1987)

Macready, Sir Nevil. *Annals of an Active Life* (George H. Doran, New York, 1925)

Mahon, Tom and Gillogly, James J. *Decoding the IRA* (Mercier Press, Cork, 2008)

Massie, Robert. *Castles of Steel: Britain, Germany and the Winning of the Great War at Sea* (Ballantine Books, New York, 2003)

Memory, F.W. *"Memory's": Being the adventures of a Newspaperman* (Cassell and Company, London, 1932)

McCarthy, Kieran. *Republican Cobh and the East Cork Volunteers Since 1913* (Nonsuch Publishing, Dublin, 2008)

—— and Christensen, Maj-Britt. *Cobh's Contribution to the Fight for Irish Freedom: 1913–1990* (Oileánn Mór Publications, 1992)

McCarthy, Kieran and Breen, Daniel. *Cork Harbour Through Time* (Amberley Publishing, Gloucestershire, 2014)

McGuire, James and Quinn, James (eds). *Dictionary of Irish Biography* (Cambridge University Press, Cambridge, 2009)

McMahon, Paul. *British Spies and Irish Rebels: British Intelligence and Ireland 1916–1945* (Boydell & Brewer, Suffolk, 2007)

Moylan, Seán. *Seán Moylan in his Own Words* (Aubane Historical Society, Cork, 2004)

Mulcahy, Risteárd. *My Father the General: Richard Mulcahy and the Military History of the Revolution* (Liberties Press, Dublin, 2009)

Murphy, Gerard. *A Most Reliable Man: The Superspy who Betrayed the IRA*

(KDP Publications, 2020)

Neeson, Eoin. *The Irish Civil War: 1922–23* (Poolbeg Press, Dublin, 1995)

Nelson, Bruce. *Irish Nationalists and the Making of the Irish Race* (Princeton University Press, Princeton, 2012)

Nolan, Liam and Nolan, John. *Secret Victory: Ireland and the War at Sea, 1914–1918* (Mercier Press, Cork, 2009)

Ó Broin, Leon. *Revolutionary Underground: The Story of the Irish Republican Brotherhood, 1858–1924* (Rowman and Littlefield, Totowa, 1976)

O'Callaghan, Seán. *Execution* (Frederick Muller, London, 1974)

Ó Conchubhair, Brian (ed). *Rebel Cork's Fighting Story 1916–21: Told by the Men Who Made It* (Cork, Mercier Press, 2010)

O'Connor Frank. *An Only Child* (Pan Books, London, 1979)

— *The Big Fellow* (Mercier Press, Cork 2018)

O'Donoghue, Florence. *No Other Law* (Anvil Books, Tralee, 1986)

— *Sworn to be Free: The Complete Book of IRA Jailbreaks: 1918–1921* (Anvil Books, Tralee, 1971)

— *Tomás MacCurtain* (The Kerryman, Tralee, 1958)

O'Flanagan, Patrick and Buttimer, Cornelius (eds). *Cork History and Society: Interdisciplinary Essays on the History of an Irish County* (Geographic Publications, Dublin, 1993)

O'Halpin, Eunan. *Defending Ireland: The Irish Free State and its Enemies Since 1922* (Oxford University Press, Oxford, 2000)

Ó Loingsigh, Padraig (ed). *The Book of Cloyne: Leabhar Chluain Uamha* (Cloyne Historical and Archaeological Society, Midleton, 1977)

O'Mahony, Colman. *The Maritime Gateway to Cork: A History of the Outports of Passage West and Monkstown from 1754–1942* (Tower Books, Cork, 1986)

O'Malley, Ernie. *On Another Man's Wound* (Dublin, Anvil Books, 1997)

— *The Men Will Talk to Me: Kerry Interviews* (Mercier Press, Cork, 2012)

— *The Men Will Talk to Me: West Cork Interviews* (Mercier Press, Cork, 2015)

— *The Singing Flame* (Anvil Books, Dublin, 1992). Reprinted by Mercier Press

O'Riordan, Patrick. *Portraiture of Cork Harbour Commissioners* (Dowling and Dowling, Cork, 2014)

Ó Ruairc, Pádraig Óg. *Revolution: A Photographic History of Revolutionary Ireland, 1913–1923* (Cork, Mercier Press, 2014)

— *Truce: Murder, Myth and the Last Days of the Irish War of Independence* (Mercier, Cork, 2016)

Pike, W.T. (ed). 'Contemporary Biographies' in Hodges, Richard, *Cork and County Cork in the Twentieth Century* (W. T. Pike and Co, Brighton, 1911)

Preston, Diana. *Lusitania: An Epic Tragedy* (Walker and Company, New York, 2002)

Regan, John M. *The Irish Counter-Revolution: 1921–1936* (Gill and Macmillan, Dublin, 1999)

— *Myth and the Irish State: Historical Problems and Other Essays* (Irish Academic Press, Sallins, 2013)

Share, Bernard. *Slanguage: A Dictionary of Irish Slang* (Dublin, Gill & Macmillan, 1997)

Ryan, Meda. *The Day Michael Collins was Shot* (Poolbeg, Dublin, 1989)

— *Tom Barry: IRA Freedom Fighter* (Mercier Press, Cork, 2003)

Ryle Dwyer, T. *'I signed my death Warrant': Michael Collins and the Treaty* (Mercier Press, Cork, 2006)

— *The Squad and the Intelligence Operations of Michael Collins* (Mercier Press, Cork, 2005)

— *Michael Collins: The Man who Won the War* (Mercier Press, Cork, 2009)

Share, Bernard. *In Time of Civil War: The Conflict on the Irish Railways, 1922–23* (The Collins Press, Cork, 2006)

Sheehan, William. *A Hard Local War: The British Army and the Guerrilla War in Cork, 1919–1921* (Spellmount, The History Press, Gloucestershire, 2011)

— *British Voices: From the Irish War of Independence 1918–1921* (The Collins Press, Cork, 2007)

Sims, Rear-Admiral William Sowden. *The Victory at Sea* (James Stevenson, Fairfield, 2002)

Steel, Nigel and Hart, Peter. *Jutland 1916: Death in the Grey Wastes* (Cassell, London, 2004)

Still, William N. (ed.). *The Queenstown Patrol, 1917: The Diary of Commander Joseph Knefler Taussig, US Navy.* (Rhode Island, Naval War College Press, 1996)

Taylor, Rex. *Michael Collins* (Four Square Books, London, 1966)

Thomas, P. N. *British Steam Tugs* (Waine Research Publications, Albrighton, 1991)

Tittoni, Senator Tommaso. *Italy's Foreign and Colonial Policy* (English translation, E. P. Dutton, New York, 1915)

Tooze, Adam. *The Deluge: The Great War, America and the Remaking of the Global Order, 1916–31* (Viking, New York, 2014)

Townshend, Charles. *The Republic: The Fight for Irish Independence* (London, Penguin Books, 2014)

Twohig, Patrick J. *Blood on the Flag* (Tower Books, Ballincollig, 1996)
— *Green Tears for Hecuba: Ireland's Fight for Freedom* (Tower Books, Ballincollig, 1994)
— *The Dark Secret of Béalnabláth* (Tower Books, Ballincollig, 1997)
Valiulis, Maryann Gialanella. *Portrait of a Revolutionary: General Richard Mulcahy and the Founding of the Irish Free State* (University Press of Kentucky, Lexington, 1992)
Vaughan, W.E. (ed). *A New History of Ireland, VI, Ireland Under the Union, II, 1870–1921* (Clarendon Press, Oxford, 1996)
War Office General Staff, *Official History of the operations in Somaliland, 1901–1904* (Harrison and Sons, London, 1907)
White, Gerry and O'Shea, Brendan. *Baptised in Blood: The Formation of the Cork Brigade of the Irish Volunteers, 1913–1916* (Mercier Press, Cork, 2005)
— *The Burning of Cork* (Mercier Press, Cork, 2006)
Who Was Who: 1929–1940 (Adam & Charles Black, London, 1967)
Younger, Calton. *A State of Disunion* (Fontana Books, London, 1972)

INDEX